To Barbara
With love from Ann

Christmas 1997

To Barbara
With love from Ann

Christmas 1997

Gardening
WITH
Silk and Gold

A HISTORY OF GARDENS
IN EMBROIDERY

Gardening
WITH
Silk and Gold

A HISTORY OF GARDENS IN EMBROIDERY

THOMASINA BECK

David & Charles

In Spring when Flow'rs your garden grace,
With Needle or Pencil you can trace
Each curious Form, and various Dye
So represent unto the Eye,
Noble proportion ev'ry Part
That Nature blushes at your Art
John Rea, *Flora*, 1665

Jacket, background embroidery *Elizabethan silk cushion
reproduced by kind permission of the Victoria & Albert Museum*

Endpapers *Part of a early seventeenth-century English long cover.
Linen embroidered with silk in long-and-short, stem, herringbone
and satin stitches with laid and couched work*

Page 1 *Detail of lovers in an arbor in a sixteenth-century valance*

Page 2 *Silk picture of a lady watering flowers c.1790*

Page 3 Girl in a Garden *by Jenny Chippindale, 1985. Patchwork
hanging in dyed and sprayed calico with surface stitchery*

Page 5 *Gardeners worked in chain stitch on satin on an
eighteenth-century French waistcoat*

A DAVID & CHARLES BOOK

First published in the UK in 1997

A catalogue record for this book is available from the British Library.

ISBN 0 7153 0487 9

Book design by Margaret Foster
Printed in Singapore by C. S. Graphics Pte Ltd
for David & Charles
Brunel House   Newton Abbot   Devon

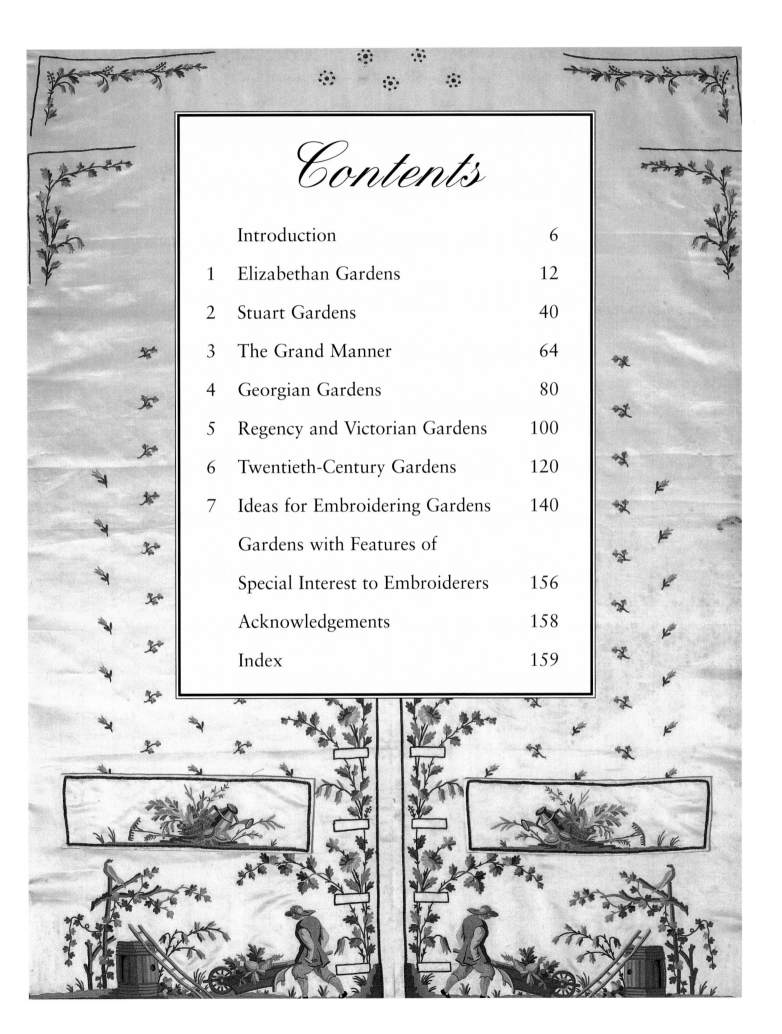

Contents

Introduction

In a lecture he gave on pattern-designing in 1881, William Morris likened embroidery to 'gardening with silk and gold thread', a poetic phrase which I have adopted as the title for this revised and updated edition of my *Embroidered Gardens (1979)* as it so perfectly expresses the affinity between gardens and embroidery. My interest in the close links between the two arts began some 25 years ago, when I noticed a small garden in the background of an Elizabethan valance in the Victoria & Albert Museum. It caught my attention at once as I was busy making a knot garden at the time, and was avidly searching for information and inspiration in old garden books. I read with particular pleasure a passage in Sir George Sitwell's *On the Making of Gardens* (1909). 'The garden,' he wrote, 'should be something without and

beyond nature; a page from an old romance, a scene in fairyland, a gateway through which the imagination, lifted above the sombre realities of life, may pass into a world of dreams…' And in a later passage he continued, 'In such scenes there is the same elusive suggestiveness that is found in the perfume of flowers… It has the power of fixing the attention, it grips you by the sleeve…you feel…that it is "seeking to communicate", to open up vistas into the past'. That tug at the sleeve was exactly what I had felt when I saw the knot garden embroidered in the valance shown on page 9. However faded, the little garden seemed somehow to communicate the spirit of the age in a strangely evocative manner, as if the embroidery possessed that same 'elusive suggestiveness' as the perfume of flowers. In such a setting the characters from *Twelfth*

Right *A romantic garden perspective by Mary Campion from Viscountess Wolseley's* Gardens their Form and Design *(1919). Her distinctive drawing style is strongly suggestive of stitchery*

Above *Flora from the title page of Mattioli's* Commentaries

Opposite *The dream-like atmosphere of Joy Real's* Florentine Garden *(1995) shows how effectively embroidery can evoke the mood of a garden. It depicts her granddaughter pensive in the gardens of Villa I Tatti on a memorable visit. Inspiration for the border came from the work of the Florentine sculptor Lucca della Robbia (1399–1482). Applied fabric with machine and hand stitchery*

Beaded panel of pansies, dated 1657

Below left *A parterre design drawn by Belinda Downes, inspired by the eighteenth-century embroidered picture shown on page 69, and* (below right) *an engraving of a Dutch garden in which the parterre is presented as a pattern rather than in perspective*

Night would have met and dallied, there would have been al fresco banquets, music and pleasant places where one might stitch and chat in summer. Soon after, I came on a small beaded cushion, also in the V&A, decorated with stylized pansies and the words 'Natures flowers soon do fade/ Full long we last cause art us made', suggesting that needlework, though itself ephemeral, can not only outlive, but faithfully record flowers – and gardens too.

The embroidered garden and the couplet on the cushion seemed to be tangible links with a vanished world, and an invitation to search for other garden scenes which might open up further 'vistas into the past'. *Gardening with Silk and Gold* describes the gardens I have found in needlework, starting in the Elizabethan age and continuing into the present; it tells of both in the words of contemporary writers, and shows how the two arts go hand in hand, each revealing in the other similar pictures, patterns and moods.

The intricate patterns and plants of the Elizabethan knot gardens were mirrored in miniature in embroidery on dress and furnishings, to be followed by the exuberant scrolling designs of the Stuart and early Georgian Grand Manner, just as well suited to a gentleman's waistcoat as

A knot garden embroidered in tent stitch in the background of an

Elizabethan valance telling the story of Myrrha (shown on page 20)

to the parterre in his garden. Then, in the eighteenth century, the pendulum of fashion moved away from formality, and landscape gardens replaced the parterres, their paths meandering as prettily as the flower stems embroidered on dresses and aprons – 'natural', but in fact most artfully contrived, and to be replaced in their turn by the 'geometrical' gardens of the Victorians, bright with carpet bedding, whose dazzling appearance was echoed in the garish colours and patterns of Berlin woolwork.

In reaction to both of these, William Morris turned back to the simplicity of the medieval flowery mead, the spirit of the Elizabethan pleasance, and the inspiration of the growing plants – roses, oaks and vines – 'those natural forms which are at once most familiar and delightful to us, as well from association as from beauty'. Embroidery like the other arts 'should remind you of something beyond itself, of something of which it is a visible symbol'. In his designs he wanted 'unmistakeable suggestions of gardens', and these are what his inimitable patterns evoke.

Later Victorian embroiderers presented the garden through pictures rather than patterns, influenced perhaps by Gertrude Jekyll, who saw garden-making as the creation of beautiful pictures. Patterns and pictures alternate in popularity in this history, as the pendulum of fashion swings from formal to informal and back again. And where is it now? Garden styles in the twentieth century have become increasingly eclectic, alternating and sometimes juxtaposing formal and informal elements, so it is no surprise to find patterns and pictures, formal and informal treatments enjoying equal popularity in garden needlework. It is crocus time as I write. In Kew Gardens, drifts of purple and white spread out under the trees, decorating the grass in as pictorial a prospect as anyone could wish. Go to Copenhagen and you will see a dramatically different crocus carpet extending in front of the Renaissance castle of Rosenborg, planted in the same

Opposite Inspired by Andrew Marvell's verse, this bookcover for Thomasina Beck's The Embroiderer's Flowers *(1992) was made by Margaret Nicholson and Heide Jenkins in 1996. Margaret designed and embroidered the flowers in* or nué, *a time-consuming and demanding method in which metal threads are laid on a background of calico marked with the design and then couched down in silk. Heide made the insects and bound the book in lilac-coloured shot silk with passementerie ties. An* or nué *fritillary set in the shape of a bulb ornaments the back of the cover*

Right Patricia Sales experiments with raised work in Tiptoe through the Tulips, *1994*

colours, but in precise blocks, creating a rich and richly satisfying geometric pattern. Which attracts you? Either could be treated representationally, or as abstract pattern; interesting perspectival effects could be tried out; those purple-shaded silks bought long ago on impulse could now spark new ideas.

Although the Danish crocus carpet looks strikingly modern, its inspiration came from Renaissance garden ideas. Interest in garden history has never been greater, and the many gardens that have been restored or re-created in period style are rich in possibilities for embroiderers. The past is waiting to be plundered, and remade for our own times. Embroidery, like gardening, is about looking – looking at how the effects, past and present, have been achieved, assessing them, seeing how they might be adapted to fit into one's own scheme of things.

Nothing gives me greater pleasure than to hear that my trilogy of books on flowers and gardens has provided useful starting points for design, and one of the reasons for updating this, the first volume, was to suggest further projects and pointers. The old patterns are infinitely renewable, and in their new drawings Paddy Killer and Belinda Downes show how the pictures, plans and plants of the past might be reworked for contemporary use. Poems, songs and phrases also play their part, lingering in the mind until suddenly they spark an idea.

The starting point for the design of the superlative book

cover shown opposite, worked in *or nué* by Margaret Nicholson and bound by Heide Jenkins, was a verse by the seventeenth-century poet Andrew Marvell:

> See how the Flowers as at Parade
> Under their colours stand displayed:
> Each regiment in order grows,
> That of the Tulip, Pink and Rose.

It was tulips again, this time in the hummable refrain from the Thirties' favourite 'Tiptoe through the Tulips', that set Pat Sales off on her embroidery of figures and flowers dancing together in celebration of tulip time. Her picture also draws inspiration from stumpwork, the raised embroidery of the seventeenth century, which she has imaginatively updated for enjoyment today. The fun of embroidery, as in gardening, lies in experimenting – experimenting with techniques, with patterns, with materials – saying 'Let's have a go and try this', and if it does not suit, working out an alternative method, in a new colour scheme and on a slightly different scale. The last chapter of this book suggests pointers for experimentation – ideas sparked off by some of the images that appear in earlier pages.

The initial point for Paddy Killer's chapter headings was the theme of music, gardens and needlework – arts which are linked by their quality of evanescence, fleeting and fading all too quickly.

Elizabethan Gardens

'All is work and nowhere space'

THOMAS CAMPION, FROM PHILIP ROSSETER'S *A BOOK OF AIRS*, 1601

ROMANCY PLEASANT PLACES

'For if delight may provoke men's labour, what greater delight is there than to see the earth aparelled with plants as in a robe of imbroidered works, set with orient pearles and garnished with great diversitie of costlie jewels,' wrote John Gerard in 1597, dedicating his *Herball* to Lord Burghley. Gerard had supervised the great stateman's magnificent garden at Theobalds near London, and his comparison of the decorative effect of embroidered dress with a profusion of growing plants could have been inspired either by the beauty of Lord Burghley's famous flower collection, or by the variety of plants which he himself grew in his own garden a few miles away in Holborn.

In the sixteenth century many writers and poets noted a resemblance between their gardens and the embroidery around them, and they would have known exactly what Gerard meant. Their gardens had rare, ornate and fanciful qualities which found a real and extraordinary parallel in the embroidery of the period. Each art then reached a perfection that has seldom been surpassed in later years, though succeeding fashions may have overshadowed their achievements. Since hardly a trace of these gardens remains for us to visit – all were destroyed or submerged in the following centuries – the surviving embroideries are not only examples of one art, but a precious record of another, the two being strangely and wonderfully related, and between them evoking the aesthetic, cultural and mysterious images of the age.

Elizabethan embroidery resembled the garden in two distinct ways. Miniature garden scenes illustrating all the

The Elizabethans' passionate enthusiasm for gardens and flowers is reflected in the title page of Gerard's Herball (opposite) *where Flora presides over a wealth of plants including old favourites and new introductions, and* (above) *in* the portrait of a lady of the Spenser family, British School, c. 1600. The aptness of Gerard's comparison of 'the earth aparelled with plants as in a robe of imbroidered works' is evident in the gorgeous stitchery of pansies, honeysuckle and strawberries set jewel-like in puffs of transparent gauze on her gown. The neat arrangement of beds in the cartouche was ideal for displaying the plants and similar layouts often occur in embroidered furnishings features then in fashion were depicted in embroidered furnishings, where every detail of the layout was clear except for the actual planting of the beds. The tiny scale of these embroideries makes it impossible to see which plants were used and how they were arranged. The plants can, however, be seen in detail on 'robes of imbroidered work', and on cushions and covers where they were arranged to create decorative effects similar to those in the garden. Herein lay the second resemblance.

The miniature scenes (see pages 16 and 18) appeared most often in the background of luxurious furnishings which were among the most exciting decorative innovations of the age. The gardens can be seen in hangings, table carpets – carpets on the floor were a rarity seen more often in portraits than in reality – and valances. The latter were long pelmet-like bands made in sets of three to hang from the roof of a four-poster bed and were ideal for narrative embroidery where the story unfolds in a series of episodes. Fortunes were spent on bed hangings, and when garden scenes were worked on the valances and bright flowers ran riot on pillows, coverlets and curtains, the whole bed echoed the garden. This may have been in Christopher Marlowe's mind when he described the interweaving of honeysuckle and rose stems over a stream as being like embroidery: 'And as a costly valance o'er a bed, So did their garland tops the brook o'erspread'.

Tent stitch in wool or silk on linen canvas was a favourite method, and many of the finest furnishings were made in professional workrooms where several embroiderers could sit round a large frame. They transformed the interiors of Elizabethan houses, making them brighter and more inviting than ever before. The embroideries were especially appealing to their owners as they brought echoes of the garden indoors to be enjoyed throughout the year, preserving flowers and sunshine, spring and summer to brighten the gloomy winter days. The gardens were not the main subject of the furnishings, but were again and again the setting for a varied cast of biblical, mythological and allegorical characters, acting out scenes from a distant legendary past, while dressed, incongruously, in the height of current fashion. The figures were frequently copied from engravings, and details of dress sometimes suggest a French origin. The copying was done by professional draughtsmen, who would enliven the foreground with an array of small animals and plants, and fill in the background around the figures with contemporary garden scenes. Here the fashions in England and France remained similar throughout the sixteenth century. If they were specially commissioned, their future owner may sometimes have asked for the scene to include a view or a glimpse of his own garden, just as his coat of arms might be incorporated into some part of the design.

Although the gardens no longer exist, vivid contemporary descriptions record them at the height of their glory. Garden visiting was as popular then as it is now, and travellers and enthusiasts expressed delight in what

Musicians serenade a couple seated in a simply constructed rose arbour in a late sixteenth-century valance. Behind them a pavilion leads into an alley with 'windows' for viewing another part of the garden

they saw. A German named Paul Hentzner who visited the gardens of Henry VIII's fantastic palace at Nonsuch in 1598 records that it was 'so encompassed with parks full of verdure, deer, delicious gardens, groves ornamented with trelliswork, and cabinets of verdure that it seems to be a place pitched upon by Pleasure to dwell in along with Health'. A year later another traveller, Thomas Platter, also went to Nonsuch, where he found Queen Elizabeth in residence. The party was conducted to the Presence Chamber, saw the Queen 'most lavishly attired in a gown of pure white satin, gold embroidered', and then, after dining, walked amid the mazes and knots of the garden.

Knots were beds laid out in elaborate interlacing patterns, planted in low clipped evergreens where 'all kinds of plants and shrubs are mingled in intricate circles as though by the needle of Semiramis'. The comparison is apt, for inside the houses the travellers visited they would have seen colourful tapestries and embroidered furnishings depicting gardens so finely stitched that they might indeed have been the work of Semiramis, the legendary Eastern queen famous for the splendour of her gardens. The embroidered scenes correspond in every detail with the written accounts, and, according to Platter, were so lifelike that 'the plants seemed to be growing indeed'. Platter also visited Hampton Court, seeing 'extremely costly tapestries worked in gold and silver so lifelike that one might take the people and plants for real'.

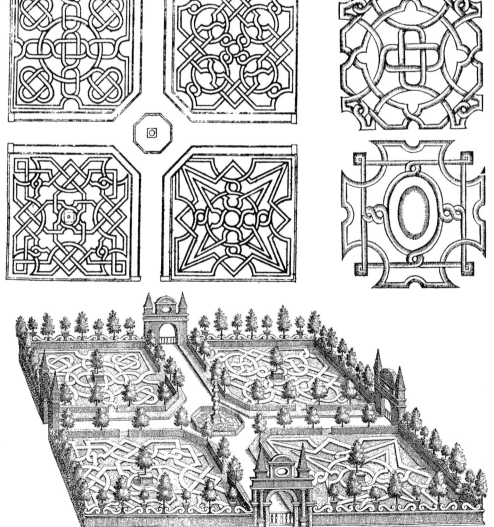

Bottom left *A bird's-eye view of a knot garden forming part of the elaborate layout designed by de Caus for the castle of Heidelberg. The plan of the garden (above left) shows the individual knot patterns. Intricate knots from Gervase Markham's* The Countrie Farme *(above right)*

Sometimes the garden theme was continued in painting, as at Theobalds where the walls of the Great Chamber were decorated with oak trees so startlingly realistic that birds flew in singing from the pleasure gardens outside to perch on the branches. Indoors seemed to be masquerading as outdoors and vice versa. The effect was delightfully ambiguous, as Barnaby Goodge remarked enthusiastically in 1577: 'Your Parlers and your banquetting houses both within and without, as all bedeckt with pictures of beautiful Flowres and Trees, that you may not only feede your eyes with the beholding of the true and lively Flowre, but also delight your selfe with the counterfaite in the middest of Winter.'

The garden in the Franklin hanging shown on this page records in miniature many of the features the travellers actually saw. A hunting park stretches away into wood-land behind the house, while in complete contrast to the animated hunting scene the garden lies peaceful, ordered and serene. It is like the transformation John Aubrey noted when he wrote that Lord Stourton had, in making his garden, converted what was 'heretofore all horrid and woody' into 'a most parkly ground and romancy pleasant place'. Here nature is dressed up as ornately and corseted as stiffly as the ladies and gentlemen in the foreground, with the garden designed to set off the house as elaborately as the ruffs framing the faces of its owners. It is partly enclosed, with a covered alley linking two pavilions and a central arbour, and is laid out with flowerbeds and circular mazes planted with evergreen shrubs and herbs such as santolina, lavender, germander and thrift. These

'intricate circles' were best appreciated from the windows or raised terrace of the house; in *The Countrie Farme*, published in 1600, Richard Surflet describes his delight in looking out over his garden, seeing 'fair and comely proportions, handsome and pleasant arbours, and as it were closets, delightful borders of lavender, rosemary, box and such like' and smelling 'so sweet a nosegay so near at hand'. The flowers and herbs in the beds not only exhaled the scent of a mixed nosegay but resembled one, with as many different plants as possible mingling their shapes, colours and textures together. In *The Merry Wives of Windsor*, Shakespeare compared the decorative effect to needlework: 'Emerald tufts, flowers purple blue and white / Like sapphires, pearls and rich embroidery'.

Opposite *The garden lies behind the moated house in the Franklin hanging, set apart from the hunting park and enhanced by elaborate carpenter's work*

Right *The patterning of knots, mazes and vineyards frames the château as decoratively as a ruff round a face in this bird's-eye view of Montargis by du Cerceau*

Detail from a set of valances telling the story of the unfortunate Philomela, whose tongue has been cut out by the cruel King of Thrace. Here in a flowery setting she embroiders a message for her sister recounting her sad fate

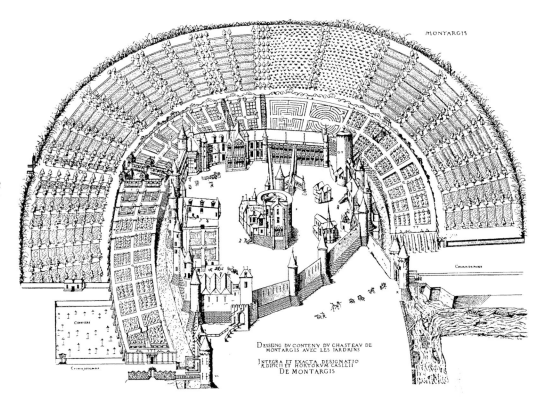

FROM CLOISTER TO PLEASURE GARDEN

The Elizabethan gardens had all the charm of novelty. Visitors even a few decades earlier, in the turbulent days before Tudor rule, would have seen nothing like them. There were gardens then, of course, but they were hidden away behind the walls of castles and monasteries, where herbs were grown for medicinal or culinary purposes. Flowers were for the decoration of the church and for weaving into garlands for festival days. The simple layout of these early gardens, with a neat chequerboard of raised beds and covered walks, can be seen small and jewel-like in illuminated manuscripts and books of hours.

The concept of the country house as the centre of an agreeable and leisurely way of life came into being in the sixteenth century, and the garden was to play an important part in the process. The garden depicted in the valance on this page retains the main features of the medieval cloister. The plan is still close to the cruciform layout with a central fountain and plants trained over a trellis frame running round the sides, but in a medieval castle or a monastery it would have been further enclosed by a high wall so that it was shut in on itself, and as inward-looking as the world of which it was a part. Now the house looks peacefully out over the countryside beyond, and the owner might see pleasant views of each as he walked in the shade of the alley and paused at one of the openings. Thomas Hill, author of the first practical books to be written in English about gardens, found them not only pleasurable to walk in but wonderfully restorative. In *The Gardener's Labyrinth* of 1577 he expresses his contemporaries' delight in gardens where the alleys and

The figure of Christ appearing to Mary Magdalene in the guise of a gardener towers over the tiny moated garden embroidered in the background of this late sixteenth-century valance. Plants trained on trellis form tunnel-like alleys enclosing a neat four-square plot *with a central fountain. The garden stands out from the landscape in its formality, and from the corner arbours, the owner could enjoy the pleasing contrast between Nature, 'dressed by Art' in the garden, and unadorned in the surrounding countryside*

walks 'serve to good purposes, the one is that the owner may diligently view the prosperitie of his herbes and flowers, the other for the delight and comfort of his wearied mind, which he may by himself or in fellowship of friendes conceyve in the delectable sightes and fragrant smelles of the flowers'.

Without gardens, 'buildings and palaces are but gross handiworks: and a man shall ever see that when ages come to civility and elegancy, men shall come to build stately sooner than to garden finely; as if gardening were the greater perfection', wrote Francis Bacon in his essay *On Gardens*, published in 1625. Himself as much an Elizabethan as a Jacobean – he was born in 1561 – Bacon was expressing Elizabethan sentiments exactly, for many cultured people then had no doubts as to their 'civility and elegancy' and the garden was ideal for showing off both qualities.

Like his house, the garden was a status symbol reflecting not only the owner's taste and wealth but also his own creative talent in a novel and pleasingly idiosyncratic manner. The owners of the new mansions and manor houses that were being built all over Britain were enthusiastically involved in the arts. They read widely, wrote, composed, sang and danced. They supervised the building, and sometimes even designed their houses themselves, indulging their taste for intricate patterning and elaborate effects in every detail of the decoration. Gardening became an accomplishment as well as being a pastime – and at exactly the same time embroidery, which had long been a necessary accomplishment, began to flourish with a new exuberance. Together, garden and embroidery combined to add the perfect finishing touch to the house and its contents. For those who, despite their 'civility and elegancy', were not quite sure how to go about the practical business of laying out a garden and cultivating the plants, books soon began to appear. The earliest was

'Silver sounding Musick, mixt instruments and Voices gracing all the rest. How you will be wrapt with Delight,' wrote William Lawson, describing the pleasurable 'Ornaments' of an orchard or garden. Scenes of music and dancing in a garden setting were often recorded in Elizabethan furnishings, as here in a late sixteenth-century valance

by Thomas Hill, published in 1563 with the lengthy title *A Most Briefe and pleasaunt treatyse, teachynge howe to sowe and set a Garden, and what propertyes also these few herbes here spoken of have to our comodytie: with the remedyes that may be used against such beasts, wormes, flies and such lyke, that commonly noy gardes* [annoy gardens]… The many 'beasts, wormes, flies and such lyke' in Elizabethan embroidery suggest that the 'remedyes' were seldom successful.

THE ROMANCE OF THE VALANCE

On Hill's title page there is a tiny woodcut of a garden set in the countryside yet enclosed on all four sides and symmetrically divided within. Its privacy and seclusion, its detailed layout and its rural situation are all typical of the Elizabethan garden, and all are repeated in a pair of valances telling the double and linked stories of Adonis and Myrrha and Venus and Adonis from Ovid's *Metamorphoses*, which had been translated from the Latin in 1567 and were enormously popular.

The story opens with the dramatic image of Myrrha on the point of hanging herself in an arbour well hidden by a luxuriant vine trained on trellis between flower-decked columns. The well-read Elizabethan would have known at once that the cause of Myrrha's distress was her incestuous passion for Cinyras, her father, who had unwisely boasted that she was more beautiful than the goddess Venus (seen

The title page of Thomas Hill's A Most Briefe and pleasaunt Treatyse *depicts a typical layout with a central knot and beds surrounded with ornamental trellis*

in the lower valance driving her swan-drawn chariot through the clouds). Myrrha's old nurse leads her from the arbour into the knot garden, and in a secluded corner outlines her plan; while his wife is away, she will administer a potion so that Cinyras will sleep with his daughter unwittingly. This transpires, and when Cinyras discovers that Myrrha is pregnant he chases her from the house; just as he is about to strike her with his sword, Venus relents and turns her into a myrrh tree whose gaping trunk reveals the baby Adonis. This second valance is much closer in theme to the two poems in which Shakespeare talks of the legend, '*The Passionate Pilgrim*' and '*Venus and Adonis*'. Neither the tale on the valances nor the poems are deeply learned, but the embroiderer has seized upon this story of thwarted amorous dalliance – an intentionally apt choice of subject for bed hangings – for the excuse it provides to depict the trials of love in a setting of rural and garden delight. In the second valance, the young Adonis has disdained the advances of Venus, choosing rather to go out hunting in the forest, but he meets and is killed by a wild boar. In the needlework, the forest is transformed into an orchard with an ornate marble fountain whose water pours into a stream running between flowery banks. Venus looks down from her chariot on the dying Adonis while a nightingale laments in the tree behind. Two details continue the garden setting: far to the rear there is a sumptuous summerhouse, similar perhaps to the one pleasantly situated upon the highest part of Nonsuch Park, from which the guests might view the hunt; and just adjacent to Venus in the clouds, there is a tiny snail-shaped mount.

Mounts, made from earth, wood or stone 'harmoniously wrought within and without' were small artificial hillocks raised up in the garden, either against the outer wall or in the centre, sometimes topped by an arbour or even a banqueting house. Whether in the centre or against the wall, they were vantage points from which to see beyond the garden into the park or countryside, or to look down onto the patterns in the knotted beds.

Mounts are rare in the embroidered garden, but the one in the Adonis valance is certainly close to the description of a mount with topiary work seen by John Leland at Wressel Park in the 1540s 'writhen about with turnings of cokilshells to come to the top without payne'. It is also similar to the 'Snayl' mount, one of three small islands rising from the large 'Pond' rapidly dug out at Elvetham in Hampshire for the entertainments put on by the Earl of Hertford for Queen Elizabeth in 1591. The Queen sat in a bower decorated with greenery and ripe hazelnuts. Both the bower and the lake had been created especially for the three-day revels during which – in true English fashion – 'it rained extremely'.

A pair of valances linking the stories of Myrrha and Adonis and Venus and Adonis. Above: *The first three episodes take place in a vine arbour, a knot garden (shown in detail on page 9, similar in layout to Thomas Hill's woodcut shown opposite) and the bedchamber of Cinyras. Below: The newly born Adonis clings to the branch of the myrrh tree, and then, in a startlingly rapid transition from baby to manhood, encounters the wild boar, is killed and then mourned over by Venus and her ladies in a garden setting with an elaborate fountain and mount*

A 'Snayl' mount 'rising to four circles of green privie [privet]' was one of the features in the 'Pond cut to the perfect figure of a half moon' for water sports at Elvetham in 1591. Fireworks exploded from the mount during the pageant

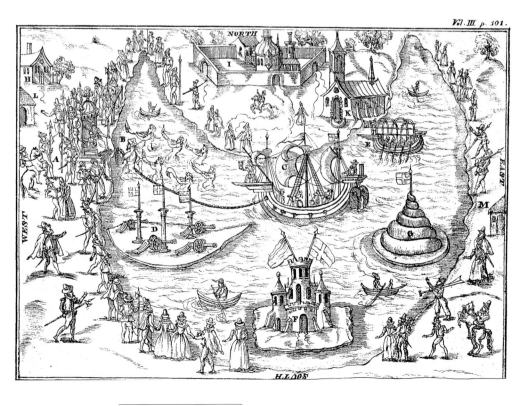

Opposite *Queen Elizabeth holding an olive branch and wearing a flower-embroidered dress in the garden at Wanstead House, painted by Marcus Gheeraerts the Elder c.1585*

Above *Carpenter's work was an essential feature in sixteenth-century gardens, creating intimate enclosures, as here in a detail of a late sixteenth-century valance at Parham Park*

MANY DELIGHTS OF RARE INVENTION

Although she did not herself make any new gardens, the Queen's summer progresses into the country to visit her courtiers made them vie with each other not only in building lavish houses but also in creating gardens which set the scene for masques and revels, for music and dancing, bathing and all kinds of sports and games. In fine weather all social activity migrated to the garden, which was decked out to match the mood of the entertainments.

The embroidered gardens seem able to catch this atmosphere of gaiety and pleasure more evocatively than the simple, rather crude woodcuts illustrating contemporary books, or the few paintings that survive. One reason may be that embroidery and tapestry have in their texture a quality of depth and softness and warmth which even the most subtle painting cannot render. They draw us into the poetic and sensuous world of gardens, which the Elizabethan and Jacobean writers so tantalizingly describe: 'for whereas every other pleasure commonly fills some one of our senses, this makes all our senses swimme with pleasure and that with infinite variety'. The truth of William Lawson's words, from his *New Orchard and Garden* of

1618, is borne out to delicious perfection in needlework scenes, for example in a valance at Parham Park in Sussex. Here a couple sit by their fountain, deep in decorous yet amorous dalliance. Around them, nature – tamed yet exuberant – offers evidence of pleasure and beauty. Behind the couple a laden fruit tree gives them shade, and in the background a leafy trelliswork arcade invites to more private scenes. The gentleman raising an eloquent arm may be gesturing towards the fountain to show the detail of the carving, but more likely he is declaring his love, for his other hand presses the lady's knee. And so the fountain scene is unperceived – by the gentleman at least – and only the spectator outside the embroidered story sees the cockerel at the lovers' feet, the gaudy peacock on the balustrade, the impudent rabbits among the knotted beds and the cupid who directs the scene. Such moments of exquisite enjoyment would have been appreciated by the Elizabethans both for their reality and their transience.

Embroidery preserves these vanished pleasances, revealing the Elizabethan love of lively colours, scents and sounds. In these valances we may still enjoy the seclusion of intimate gardens and imagine the fragrance of the roses

entwined so luxuriantly in the trelliswork. The scenes recall lines from a sonnet by Bartholomew Griffin:

See where my Love sits in the beds of spices,
Beset all round with camphor, myrrh and roses,
And interlaced with curious devices,
Which her from all the world apart incloses.
There does she tune her lute for her delight,
And with sweet music makes the ground to move.

Music in gardens appears again and again as a theme in embroidery, as if the transience of the one could be preserved in the other. Though embroidery lasts longer than the flowers it portrays, it too has an ephemeral quality, since the freshness of its colours fades, fleeting like the sounds of music and the fragrance of flowers. In 'Venus and Adonis' Shakespeare wrote: 'Fair flowers that are not gathered in their prime / Rot and consume themselves in little time'; and in Sonnet V, 'But Flowers distill'd though they with winter meet/ Leese but their show, their substance still lives sweet.'

Elizabethan embroidery was part of summer's distillation, conserving the essence of the flowers, and the appearance of the garden at its zenith. In the French valance on this page the knotted beds are bright with summer flowers, and a table spread with sweetmeats waits invitingly at the entrance to an alley in 'carpenter's work'. This wooden framework interwoven with plants was indispensable in Renaissance gardens, providing dappled shade for walking or sitting and for enjoying all the activities which came outside during the summer months, when the garden

Above *'If music be the food of love play on,' sighs the Duke in the opening line of* Twelfth Night, *soliloquizing on the sweet but swiftly fading sound 'that breathes upon a bank of violets/ Stealing and giving odour'. Here a lady playing a lute is worked on a late sixteenth-century tent stitch book cover*

Below *Garden visiting was already all the rage in the sixteenth century, as seen in this French valance where King Solomon shows off the fountain in his knot garden to the Queen of Sheba. A feast awaits them, laid out on a table with a gold-fringed cloth in the shade of the covered alley*

Right *The construction of carpenter's work alleys and arbours is clearly shown in this woodcut from* The Gardener's Labyrinth. *The gardener on the left is training the flowering plants onto a simple framework similar to the one depicted in the Solomon and Sheba valance above*

was used as a decorative extension to the house. Its insubstantial and airy qualities were admirably suited to the light-hearted mood of the garden and open-air entertainments. Books like Thomas Hill's *The Gardener's Labyrinth* showed exactly how it should be constructed. Using carpenter's work, amazing transformations could be achieved almost overnight, and all manner of theatrical effects created. It is not surprising that Shakespeare set so many scenes in gardens of this kind where hidden meeting-places abounded. Thus in *Twelfth Night* (Act 2 sc 5) Maria and her friends hide in a box arbour waiting for Malvolio to

The highly decorative effect of carpenter's work can be seen both in the garden and in the fanciful rose-entwined pavilion framing the view in this late sixteenth-century Brussels tapestry. Simpler carved figures can be seen in the Franklin hanging

The twining habit of honeysuckle and vines made them ideal arbour plants. Here they are formalized in a printer's device

find their spurious letter, which purports to come from Olivia; and in *Much Ado About Nothing* (Act 3 sc 1), Hero and Leander walk up and down the alleys talking in loud voices knowing that Beatrice can overhear them from the bower, 'Where honeysuckles, ripened by the sun/ Forbid the sun to enter'. The Elizabethans perfected the art of living out of doors, making the most of warmth and sun: 'For never resting time leads summer on / To hideous winter, and confounds him there' (Sonnet V).

With carpenter's work, imitations of the long galleries and cabinets of the house could easily be created out in the fresh air. In place of hangings, the walls were decked with living greenery, and the garden compartments came to resemble a series of rooms. Indoors and outdoors echoed each other. Inside, the patterns and plants of the garden were repeated in plasterwork, painting and panelling, and outdoor scenes embellished hangings in galleries and chambers.

In smaller gardens carpenter's work was no more elaborate than the rustic arbour or pergola of today, but in the gardens of the great, it reached levels of splendour and complexity reminiscent of fairy palaces. Some idea of its elaborateness can be seen in the garden tapestries made in France and the Netherlands in the late sixteenth century. In these, as in the Franklin hanging, the garden is set within an idyllic landscape, but stands out from it through its sophistication and artifice.

The idea of gardens within a garden particularly appealed to the Elizabethans, with their love of intricate effects and ingenious surprises. Carpenter's work was ideal for partially screening the view, while allowing tempting glimpses into other parts of the garden. It added mystery to the scene, making one guess at what lay beyond, just as in fashionable dress the lightest of silk gauze veiled the gorgeous material beneath, or a network of slashes on sleeve or mantle only partly revealed a further layer of richly decorated stuff.

The ornamental gardens generally lay on the far side of the house and fitted into a square or rectangular area with the best windows overlooking them. A wide terrace lay below these windows, and steps led down to broad paths dividing the garden into various compartments. Each section was complete in itself and separated from the next by a hedge or alley, or, as in William Lawson's plan (published in 1618, but still representative of an Elizabethan design), by a change in level. Here six main sections on three levels

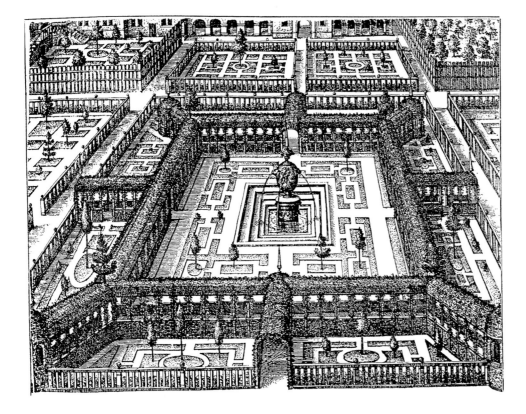

This view from Vredemann de Vries' Hortorum viridariorumque formae (1583) shows how carpenter's work divided the garden into compartments connected by covered alleys, each one having a slightly different layout

Opposite This valance detail shows a well-trimmed arbour and fountain pool. Apparently innocent fountain figures were sometimes 'full of concealed pipes which spurt upon all who come within reach'

A. Al these squares must be set with Trees, the Garden and other Ornaments must stand in spaces betwixt the Trees, and in the borders and fences.
B. Trees twenty yards asunder.
C. Garden Knots.

D. Kitching Garden.
E. Bridge.
F. Conduit.
G. Stairs.

H. Walkes set with great wood thicke.
I. Walks set with great wood round about your Orchard.
K. The Out fence.
L. The Out fence set with stone-fruit.

M. Mount. To force Earth for a Mount or such like, set it round with quicke, and lay boughes of Trees strangely intermingled, the tops inward, with the Earth in the middle.
N. Still-house.
O. Good standing for Bees, if you have an house.

P. If the River run by your door, and under your Mount, it will be pleasant.

William Lawson's pictorial plan from A New Orchard and Garden *(1618) shows a garden laid out on three levels with still-houses in each corner*

A fisherman angling 'a peckled trout' recorded in the Bradford table carpet

are reached by a bridge across a little river. Two of the sections represent ornamental orchards, and the jaunty horse and its owner represent topiary work. 'Your Gardiner can frame the lesser wood to the shape of men armed in the field ready to give battel: or swift running grey Hounds, to chase the Deere, or hunt the Hare. This kinde of hunting shall not waste your corne, nor much your coin.'

The Tudor rose stands for the knot garden, and at the bottom both the 'kitching' gardens were to be laid out decoratively with a neat arrangement of beds. Different views of the garden could be enjoyed from the mounts sited at the four corners. 'In my opinion,' wrote Lawson, 'I could highly recommend your orchard, if either through it or hard by it there should run a pleasant river with silver streams. You might sit in your Mount and angle a peckled Trout, sleighty Eele, or some other dainty Fish.' Features of his garden spring to life in many of the embroidered scenes, and its design corresponds almost exactly with a description of a garden on different levels written by Sir Henry Wotton, James I's ambassador to Venice: 'I have seene a Garden... into which the first Accesse was a high walke like a Terrace, from whence might bee taken a generall view of the whole Plott below, but rather in delightful confusion than with any plaine distinction of the pieces. From this the Beholder descending many steps, was afterwards conveyed againe, by severall mountings and valings, to various entertainments of his scent and sight: which I shall not need to describe (for that they were poeticall), let me onely note this, that every one of these diversities was as if hee had beene Magically transported into a new Garden.'

The 'delightful confusion' was probably created by the variety of patterns in the knots, and the miscellany of flowers planted in them. This effect must have particularly struck Sir Henry in contrast to the symmetrical designs he would have seen in Italy, where water, stone and greenery combined to make magnificent formal settings for villas, and flowers were relegated to a separate 'secret garden'. In Elizabethan England flowers were given pride of place, grown not only in knots but in beds and borders along the walls, and informally on grassy banks and beside the streams.

AN INFINITE VARIETIE OF SWEET SMELLING FLOWERS

Flowers also appealed for their virtues and properties, and all kinds of mysterious, magical and emblematic associations. For the Elizabethans it was as if, standing on the terrace overlooking the gardens, they had before them not only in Lawson's words 'an infinite varietie of sweet smelling flowers decking with sundrie colours the green mantle of the earth', but a living treasury, ready to fill cosmetic boxes, medicine chests, still-rooms and store cupboards.

A man's nightcap with a lavender-like design by Thomas Trevelyon

Almost every plant had special properties, often mysterious or curative. William Turner, for example, in his *Newe Herball* of 1551 recommended spikes of lavender: 'quilted in a cap and dayly worne they are good for all diseases of the head that do come from a cold cause and they comfort the brain very well'. Not only caps but gloves and other garments too were delicately scented with perfumes made from the flowers whose likeness was embroidered upon them. Beliefs in these properties affected all parts of gardening, from the choice of flowers and their almost magical properties to the growing and gathering of them: for example 'Lyllies and Roses planted together will both smell the pleasanter because of their aimiable disposition', whereas the ranunculus is 'of a very unsociable Nature and will not thrive mixed or standing next to any other sort'. Well into the seventeenth century, farmers and gardeners in England were inclined to consider not merely the seasons and the weather when planting and sowing, but the phases of the moon. Thomas Hill considered the moon's influence to be the most important factor.

Interest in plants increased with the developing science of botany, and collectors competed for varieties coming in from abroad. It was the 'delectable variety' of the plants that was shown off in the garden beds, set out individually as if in one of the new botanic gardens. The apparent confusion of mixed flowers was controlled and ordered by

Peculiarly shaped plants like the mandrake fascinated Renaissance gardeners, as shown here in Den Groten *Herbarius (1533), where it appears in the guise of male and female figures*

At Hatfield House the sunken knot garden can be viewed from the surrounding grassy banks, whose mille-fleur effect contrasts with the crisp patterns of box framing the garden plants. Topiary, a fountain and a maze complete the effect, making it rich in design ideas for modern embroiderers

the dwarf evergreen borders outlining the beds. The beds and borders were themselves arranged within a regular framework so that the garden combined formal and informal elements in a blend particularly seductive to English taste.

Through most of the sixteenth century, these borders were in lavender, germander, santolina (cotton lavender), hyssop, thyme and rosemary. Box edgings, easier to maintain but less pleasantly fragrant, were a fashion brought in from Europe after 1600. This kind of ordered profusion has been re-created in the beautiful four-square knot garden in front of the Old Palace at Hatfield House, made in the true spirit of the originals. A most inviting collection of flowers is planted in the compartments of each of three knots (the fourth is a maze), tempting the visitor to explore them more closely, and then drawing the attention from one knot to the next. This enticement is paralleled in the embroidery that flourished on dress and furnishings.

ROBES OF IMBROIDERED WORK

Embroidery was worked to cover the entire ground in intricate patterns, many of them small-scale replicas of the knots in the garden. The aptness of Gerard's likening 'the earth apparrelled with plants' to 'a robe of imbroidered work' can be appreciated at once by comparing one of the knots in a rare gardening book of 1592 with an embroidery pattern from Thomas Trevelyon's *Miscellany* of 1608, both based on a motif of interlacing hearts. The two designs look remarkably similar, and the resemblance would have been all the more striking when the embroidery pattern was stitched in blackwork or coloured silks and gold and the garden knot planted out in neatly clipped evergreens. Only the curious tree roots and shoots round the edge of

Opposite Elizabethan garden and embroidery designs of striking similarity. Interlacing hearts appear (bottom left) in a knot garden design from A Short Instruction..., *in a blackwork pattern by Thomas Trevelyon (bottom right), and on a red satin cushion (above) where they frame 21 exquisitely formalized plants worked in silks, wire and metal strip and silver gilt thread*

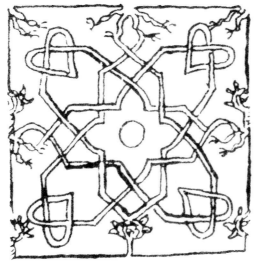

the knot garden design identify it for what it is; it would work equally well in embroidery, and conversely the needlework interlace could easily be adapted as a garden knot – perhaps with a standard honeysuckle in the centre and marigolds in the corner beds.

Garden and embroidery designs were indeed completely interchangeable, as we can see from the knots at Barnsley House in Gloucestershire and the bookbinding worked by Princess Elizabeth for her stepmother Katherine Parr in 1544. The silver knot in the latter is in braid stitch with the corners embellished with pansies, said to be the princess's favourite flower, included for their emblematic significance and perhaps also because the spaces looked as if they needed filling. This crowded intensity of patterning

The knots at Barnsley House (above) *re-create an early seventeenth-century design and are trimmed 'to a hair', so the unders and overs of the pattern are as precise as in the interlace embroidered on Princess Elizabeth's book cover* (right)

appealed equally to the taste of embroiderers and gardeners, and the opening verse of Thomas Campion's poem of 1601 applies to both their creations:

> And would you see my mistress' face
> It is a flowery garden place,
> Where knots of beauty have such grace
> That all is work and nowhere space.

The verse is charmingly illustrated in the picture shown above of Lettice Newdigate standing by a garden, the knot and interlacing patterns on the bodice of her dress echoed in the square beds of the knot garden behind her. Both the needlework and the garden knot intrigue the eye with their complexity, bringing alive the description written in 1557 of the knots at Hampton Court that were 'so enknotted it cannot be exprest'. The most intricate patterns showed to the best advantage when the knot was set out in neatly clipped evergreens on sand, gravel or some other inert material; it was then called a 'closed' knot, complete in itself, to distinguish it from an 'open' one in which flowers filled the spaces.

A beautiful embroidered version of an open knot can be

A portrait of Lettice Newdigate (redrawn by Belinda Downes) shows her holding a posy of flowers and a butterfly. She wears a 'robe of imbroidered work' whose intricate patterns are repeated in the knots glimpsed in a garden overlooked by dome-shaped arbour. Similar knots appear (top right) in Jane Bostocke's sampler and (bottom right) in a knot design from Gervase Markham's The Countrie Farme. In his opinion the interlacing threads of the knot made it look as if it were made of 'divers coloured ribands'

seen in a red velvet cushion recorded in the inventory taken in 1601 of the possessions of Bess of Hardwick, Countess of Shrewsbury, at Hardwick Hall, built in the 1590s. A miscellany of flowers and fruit is applied to the velvet, little sprigs or slips set in an interlacing strapwork pattern. The bold outline resembles not only a garden knot but the tracery in stone crowning the roofline of the mansion and the patterns in plaster, wood and stone in the rooms inside. The interlace pattern is applied in cloth of silver, and the spaces are as curiously shaped as those in the patterns illustrated in books like William Lawson's

The Country Housewife's Garden. The single sprigs within them reflect the Elizabethans' interest in individual flowers, and their pleasure in picking, wearing and arranging nosegays to 'beautifie and refresh the house', and strewing the floor with the clippings from the hedges in the knot gardens. Both sprigs and nosegays appear over and over again in Elizabethan portraits, held in the hand or pinned near the face beside their embroidered counterparts. They were chosen for their scent, to override less pleasant smells, and for their beauty and significance. John Gerard and the other herbalists always noted which flowers were best for picking. March violets, for example, were perfect for 'Garlands for the head, Nosegays and posies, which are delightfull to looke on, and pleasant to smell to, speaking nothing of their appropriate virtues…' In this poetic passage he expresses his contemporaries' delight in flowers, which 'through their beautie, varietie of colour, and exquisite forme, doe bring to the liberall and gentlemanly minde, the remembrance of honestie, comeliness and all kinds of vertues'.

Flowers were often used indoors to scent and brighten the rooms. Livimus Lemnus, a Dutchman who visited England in the 1560s, noted the refreshing effect of cut herbs strewn in chambers and parlours, and was delighted by the sweet-smelling nosegays of mixed flowers in bedchambers and privy rooms. If, at the end of the century, he had visited Hardwick Hall, he would have been able to admire the real flowers' embroidered counterparts in almost every room, as Bess of Hardwick was not only one of the most ardent builders of the age, but also a great needlewoman. Many of the cushions, table carpets and other furnishings that were such a feature of the interior decoration of the mansion are still there; even though they have lost their original freshness, they still evoke the life and times of their creator in a unique and spellbinding manner.

Bess could call on professional help in the drawing out

The flower slips are set like jewels on this red velvet cushion cover at Hardwick Hall

If it were laid out in silver-leaved santolina or lavender, this knot from William Lawson's The Country Housewife's Garden *would resemble the Hardwick cushion*

of her designs, and part of the pleasure lay in searching for suitable motifs in the herbals and in the newly published natural history and emblem books whose intriguing illustrations were sometimes so suggestive of patterns. She clearly found the woodcuts in the *Commentaries* of the Italian herbalist Pietro Andrea Mattioli much to her taste, as herbs and vegetables as well as flowers from his books were adapted for her to work. They were drawn out in ink on fine linen canvas and then shaded prettily in tent stitch. Some were worked as small panels intended for mounting on hangings, but a favourite method was to work individual motifs of flowers, birds, animals and people in tent stitch and then cut them out from the linen and apply them to a rich ground of satin or velvet. A red satin hanging at

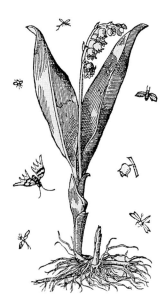

A lily of the valley from d'Aléchamps (right) *and mushrooms* (left) *from Mattioli's* Commentaries, *which were adapted for an embroidery design at Hardwick Hall*

Hardwick shows how the motifs, known as 'slips', were assembled without any thought of realistic scale, with trees smaller than flowers and plants larger than people. Much in the same manner, flowers growing between trees only slightly larger than themselves are depicted on the opening page of d'Aléchamps' *Historia Generalis Plantarum* of 1598. The effect resembles an embroidery design, and would be as easy to adapt for a cushion or valance today as it was then.

One of the loveliest Elizabethan cushions (preserved in

(Above) *Chapter heading from d'Aléchamps' plant history, with flowers rivalling the trees in size. Similar discrepancies of scale add to the fanciful effect seen in this* detail of a hanging at Hardwick (drawn by Belinda Downes) *embroidered with slips of flowers, birds, animals and people, including a lute player and lovers in an arbour*

Insects flutter among the fruit and flowers and small creatures fill the spaces on this long cushion. The slips are arranged to show off the individual qualities of the plants, as in the bed illustrated in The Gardener's Labyrinth *(right)*

the Victoria & Albert Museum) is ornamented with slips of flowers, grapes and gourds applied in neat rows on a black velvet ground. The cushion is edged with green silk fringe and corner tassels, and the decorative effect is remarkably similar to the flowerbeds depicted in Thomas Hill's woodcut, with their neat edging of boards and carved corner finials. The way the flowers are set out recalls a phrase from William Lawson's *New Orchard and Garden*, where he describes the plants 'by the skill of the gardener so comelily and orderly placed in your borders and squares and so intermingled that none looking thereon cannot but wonder to see what Nature corrected by Art can do'.

The slips share the simple yet decorative appeal of the

plants illustrated in *La Clef des Champs* by the Huguenot Jacques Le Moyne de Morgues, published in 1586. The woodcuts of flowers, fruit and vegetables in this charming pattern book provide exactly the decorative yet uncluttered outline the embroiderer prefers, and the pricking round the motifs in the copy in the British Museum speaks eloquently of the owner of the book's impatience to show off her skill in the working of such appealing motifs.

Le Moyne also painted exquisite watercolours, which illustrate perfectly the delicacy, fragility and minuteness of the flowers which the Elizabethan embroiderer endeavoured to capture. Many of the best-loved garden flowers had been brought in from the 'bank where the wild thyme blows,/ Where oxlip and the nodding violet grows', or

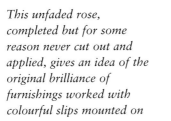

This unfaded rose, completed but for some reason never cut out and applied, gives an idea of the original brilliance of furnishings worked with colourful slips mounted on lustrous satin or velvet, like the cushion shown left (Top right) *Watercolour of a rose by Jacques Le Moyne de Morgues and a woodcut from* La Clef des Champs (bottom right)

from meadows, wood and riverside. Small and unpretentious in their natural form, honeysuckle, wild strawberries, daffodils and pinks were taken up like so many jewels by the embroiderer, who could 'correct Nature', and exaggerate the decorative qualities of the plants, making them more brilliant and 'curious' to suit the age's taste for artifice and ambiguity. With their attendant dragonflies and creepy-crawlies, the flowers embroidered on the black velvet cushion evoke the 'gay gardens' described in Edmund Spenser's *Muiopotmos* in which a butterfly flutters happily over the beds:

> There lavish Nature, in her best attire,
> Powres forth sweet odours and alluring sightes;
> And Arte, with her contending, doth aspire
> T'excell the naturall with made delights;
> And all, that faire and pleasant may be found
> In riotous excesse doth here abound.

> There he arriving round about doth flie,
> From bed to bed, from one to other border,
> And takes survey with curious busy eye,
> Of every flowre and herbe there set in order:
> Now this, now that he tasteth tenderly,
> Yet none of them he rudely doth disorder;
> Nor with his feete their silken leaves deface
> But pastures on the pleasures of each place.

'T'excell the naturall with made delights' was exactly the intention of the Elizabethan needlewomen, each with 'curious busy eye', making complex patterns and messages composed of flowers and herbs; and though these ladies, famous or unknown, are now dead and gone, we may still enjoy the 'silken leaves', knots and flowers of their embroidery.

KNOTS AND MAZES

Complexity, like 'delectable variety', was greatly admired by the Elizabethans whether in speech, dress or decoration, and of all the garden patterns the most complex was the maze. In embroidery these intricate designs were paralleled in needlemade lace and in the exquisitely fine stitchery in black silk (blackwork) ornamenting fashionable dress. While the lord of the manor set out to amuse and confuse his guests with a maze 'to sport in at times', his wife puzzled out the path of the thread in mazes of cutwork and laces, or in the labyrinthine convolutions of blackwork.

The mazes and knots recorded in furnishings were simpler in layout than the designs in contemporary manuals, and anyone using them today would be advised to make the same adjustments! A pleasing example can be seen in a valance in the Ashmolean Museum in Oxford, depicting a garden laid out in compartments, with a boy

spectator, leading him or her on to explore the twists and turns of the path and all they conceal and reveal. They remind me of the hero in du Bartas' *Divine Weeks*, published in 1584:

> Musing anon through crooked walks he wanders
> Round winding rings and intricate meanders,
> False guiding paths, doubtful beguiling strays,
> The right-wrong errors of an endless maze.

Blackwork was either worked in tiny geometric patterns on the counted thread of the background fabric or in a speckling technique where minute stitches resemble the shading of an engraving. Coiling patterns, so favoured by embroiderers and repeatedly used well into the seventeenth century, have the feeling of an 'endless maze' spreading all over the surface of the material as you would expect in a textile design, although in the pillow cover shown opposite, the border controls the 'delightful confusion' and 'delectable variety' within with neatly alternating vine leaves and grapes. In the cover the embroiderer has produced a *tour de force* of invention and ingenuity in which the twisting stems of the vine lead to different parts of the design, where each leaf encloses a new pattern and visual surprises abound. Once again 'all is work and nowhere space'.

in a balletic pose in the centre of one of the knots. Perhaps the pattern drawer was familiar with the mazes illustrated in Thomas Hill's *The Proffitable Arte of Gardening*, where a lone figure stands in the middle of each design. Almost identical mazes to those in Hill's book were the central feature in the layout at the Château of Gaillon in the 1570s. This garden was as famous in the sixteenth century as Versailles was to become in the seventeenth. The mazes and knots, each with its individual intricacy, are held together in the walled enclosure of the complete garden, so that the owner may look into the whole area to see the beds and to watch his guests as they admire the knots, or puzzle out their path within the low hedges of the maze. And this intricacy is echoed in the squares of delicate cutwork, each different and each intriguing, which were assembled into the elaborate unity of fashionable ruffs.

Hill recommends his maze to be laid out with hyssop and thyme, or with winter savory and thyme, 'for these do well endure, all the winter through grene'. The pleasing monochrome effect of these designs is paralleled in blackwork, where complex patterns engage and intrigue the

CHAPTER 2

Stuart Gardens

'There is no excellent beauty that hath not some strangeness in the proportion'
FRANCIS BACON, *ESSAY XLIII 'OF BEAUTY'*, 1625

FLORAES PARADISE

The gardens and embroidery of the early seventeenth century became increasingly elaborate. This was the age of the prodigy houses and their splendid gardens; horticultural fervour was intense, and noblemen and rich merchants vied with each other in the variety and novelty of their plant collections. Jacobean gardens like the one at Hatfield House,

built in 1611 for Lord Burghley's son Robert Cecil, 1st Earl of Salisbury, were laid out with more compartments, more fountains and more complex waterworks, while fashionable dress at the court of James I was encrusted and overlaid with a sparkling profusion of gold and silver thread, ribbons and spangled rosettes which were as intricately frilled as the most cunningly cultivated double roses and gillyflowers.

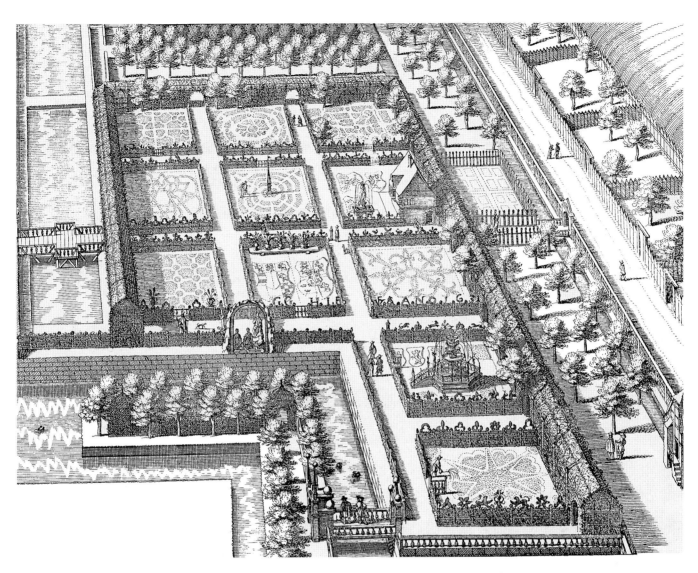

Opposite *The garden depicted in the Album Amicorum* of Gervasius Fabricius *of Salzburg, dated 1613, provides a pleasant setting for embroidery, lace-making and music. Early seventeenth-century gardens retained fountains, covered alleys and flower-filled knots of the previous age*

Above *Knots remained in fashion well into the seventeenth century, as recorded in the elaborate layout of the pleasure gardens at Hessem engraved by M. Merian. Fanciful topiary shapes* (below left) *including animals, the owners' initials (in front of their coats of arms) and the date, 1631, crown the*

trellis round each enclosure. Instructions (below right) *showing how to create these effects were given in Gervase Markham's edition of* The Countrie Farme *of 1616. As the plants grew up they would cover the framework and eventually be clipped into three-dimensional shapes along the top*

The brilliant embroidery on the jacket worn by Margaret Laton for her portrait, painted c.1610, is as fancifully conceived as a banquet of growing flowers. Roses, honeysuckle and pinks spring from a single coiling stem as if on a magical plant inhabited by vivid parakeets, butterflies and snails. The gaiety and sparkle of the bespangled blooms contrast with the crisp white geometry of the ruff, echoing the garden contrast of bright flowers and cool shimmering water made to play in patterns from the fountain jets

Court masques and ingeniously contrived theatrical effects delighted the Jacobeans just as much as they had the Elizabethans. 'Fantasticall conceits' to amuse both host and guests at such revels were described by Sir Hugh Platt in *Floraes Paradise*, which first appeared in 1608. How often were his instructions for making 'flowers candied as they grow' actually carried out? On a hot summer's morning, as soon as the dew was dry, balm, sage or borage were moistened with a mixture of gum and rosewater, and then sprinkled with fine sugar from a specially made box 'holding a paper under each flower to receive the sugar that falleth by, and in three hours it will candie or harden upon; and so you may bid your friends after dinner to a growing banquet'. Alternatively, the host could intrigue his guests with 'flowers and leaves gilded and growing' contrived in the same way, but covered with

Mid-seventeenth-century tent stitch panel of a lady in an arbour entwined with multi-flowering plants. The simultaneous appearance of sun, moon, rainbow and clouds heightens the effect of a wonderland

Below *When different climbers were trained over trelliswork the effect could resemble that of a multi-flowering plant. Arbours twined about with fruit, nuts and flowers on a single stem were a feature in Stuart needlework, seen here in a pattern inked ready for working*

gold leaf instead of sugar. They would 'remain faire notwithstanding the violence of the rain'.

Such sparkling and festive conceits would have been the perfect decorative complement to the costume of those taking part in the entertainments. The dress of both ladies and gentlemen was embroidered on sumptuous silk, satin and velvet grounds with a dazzling array of flowers, fruit, birds, insects and other devices worked in bright silks and brilliant metal threads which must have glittered as appealingly as the crystallized confections in *Floraes Paradise*. Furnishings were equally gorgeous, and contemporary inventories read like a cross between a jeweller's and a plantsman's catalogue. Among those listed in the Earl of Northampton' s inventory at the time of his death in 1614 were numerous 'paires of pillow covers', one 'embroidered with waterlilly leaves, kinges fishers and other birds and flowers of silk and gold', another ' with a running worke of pomegranates, grapes and roses silke and golde' and a third with 'a trailworke of sundrie flowers, strawberries and pinckes'.

The trailing and coiling patterns of blackwork were also worked in coloured silks and silver-gilt thread, as they had been in the previous century, and they enlivened furnishings and dress with ever more fanciful decoration. The many different blooms apparently growing from a single stem were echoed in the real alleys and arbours of the garden where plants were still carefully trained on trelliswork – as shown in the illustration in Gervase

Right Plants growing on trellis can be seen in the title page of Johann Sibmacher's pattern book of 1604. Three decades later the same title page and many of the patterns were reused by James Boler in The Needle's Excellency (below). *It is interesting that while the garden and the figure of Industry remain unchanged the dress of Wisdom and Folly have been updated, suggesting that fashions in gardens and embroidery change more slowly than in some other arts like dress*

Markham's *The Countrie Farme*. The plants would soon mingle and interweave to create the illusion of a single, many-flowered plant just as they did in embroidery. 'You shall set white thorne, eglantine and sweet briar mixt together and as they shall shoot and grow up so shall you wind and pleach them within the lattice work making them grow and cover the same.' Vines and peas were set among the climbing flowers, and they too can be seen on the coiling stems of needlework.

Plants trained on a simple trellis fence can be seen on the title page of *The Needle's Excellency,* a popular pattern book published by James Boler in 1631. Here Industry exemplifies the pleasure and profit of embroidery seated at work in a garden with pots of flowers set out on small raised beds. The book contained cutwork designs (like those on Margaret Laton's ruff and cuffs on page 42) as intricate as the garden knots in contemporary manuals, but the embroiderer, inspired by John Taylor's introductory poem, might well be eager to vary her subjects:

Flowers, Plants and Fishes, Beasts, Birds, Flyes and Bees,
Hills, Dales, Plaines, Skies, Seas, Rivers and Trees;
There's nothing neere at hand, or furthest sought,
But with the needle may be shaped and wrought.

Sadly cutwork patterns were no help with the rendering of 'flowers, plants and fishes' and if the embroiderer were to realize John Taylor's suggestions she would have to look elsewhere for designs – in Richard Shoreleyker's *A Schole-house for the Needle*, published in 1624, for example, where there were 'sundrie sorts of spots [motifs] as Flowers, Birds and Fishes', which would enable her to 'compose many faire workes'.

The simple but spirited motifs could be arranged in all sorts of decorative combinations 'according to her skill and understanding'.

By the middle of the century there were many more motifs to choose from. Delectable 'Flowers, fruits, Beasts, Birds and Flies' appeared in sheets of patterns, sold either

singly or in collections at the London print shops, and there were also picture books of popular bible stories and sheets depicting allegorical and royal characters. The pictures and motifs were adapted by professional pattern-drawers or by the embroiderers themselves to create scenes frequently set in endearingly childlike gardens in which the same flowers and features constantly reappear. These elements were to be found in real gardens, an indication that the embroiderers were influenced by the illustrations and information in garden books and by the gardens they themselves enjoyed.

The best-loved garden book of the seventeenth century was John Parkinson's *Paradisi in Sole Paradisus Terrestris, or A Garden of all Sorts of Pleasant Flowers*, published in 1629 and dedicated to Queen Henrietta Maria. The title page shows Adam apparently grafting a fruit tree in the Garden of Eden. The tree is no taller than the nearby lily, and Adam himself looks tiny beside the luxuriant carnation beside him. These discrepancies of scale, even more surprising in some of the printed sheets of patterns,

The title page of Parkinson's Paradisi in Sole Paradisus Terrestris *shows Adam and Eve cultivating native and 'outlandish' plants in the Garden of Eden*

A bird on a branch from A Schole-house for the Needle

Fruit motifs published by Peter Stent, one of the foremost London printsellers

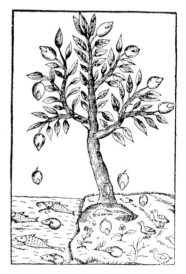

Left *Bookbinding for the Holy Bible and Book of Common Prayer printed in 1607, showing the rivers flowing out of Eden under a glittering group of patterned rocks. The scale is as strange as in the title page of the* Paradisus Terrestris

Opposite *Mid-seventeenth-century picture of Adam and Eve worked by Anne Ellys in tent, brick, and long and short stitches enlivened with silver gilt purl and spangles*

The Scythian lamb (bottom), *and* (above) *an extraordinary tree whose leaves were believed to turn into fish if they fell on water and birds if they fell on land, from C. Duret's* Histoire admirable des Plantes *of 1605*

recur in embroidery throughout the century. The Garden of Eden appealed strongly as a fanciful and decorative theme which enabled the embroiderer to assemble all manner of weird and wonderful animals, fish and insects among the marvellous plants described in books such as Parkinson's. Variations on the theme were worked, using various methods on all sorts of different articles, such as bookbindings, pillow covers and pictures, the latter an innovation unthought of in Elizabethan times when all embroidered items were intended to be used.

Despite advances in all the sciences, old superstitions and beliefs still lingered on in seventeenth-century minds, and the borderline between fact and fiction was often confused. On Parkinson's title page, an animal hangs

limply on a stem or small trunk growing out of the ground. This is the 'Scythian lamb', a creature reported in imaginative descriptions of the Far East, which was said to burst from a bud on the plant and wither away when it had eaten up the grass around it. This naïve and fantastic tale was devised to explain the white woolly heads of the cotton plant (*Gossypium herbaceum*), which had not yet been introduced to the West, and tantalized the imagination like the mermaids and other strange creatures in the pools of the embroidered gardens.

Parkinson described his book as a 'Garden of all Sorts of Flowers which our English Ayre will permit to be nursed up', and the tenderness with which he speaks of his plants suggests that he thought of them as children, needing his constant affection and attention. John Rea expressed much the same idea in his *Flora* of 1665. 'It is impossible,' he wrote, 'to have any considerable Collection of Plants to prosper unless he love them: for neither the goodness of the Soil, nor the advantages of the Situation, will do it, without the Master's affection; it is that which animates, and renders them strong and vigorous; without which they will languish and decay through neglect, and soon cease to do him service.'

The affectionate response was summed up by Parkinson when he referred to his book as a 'speaking Garden where the many herbs and flowers with their fragrant sweet smells do comfort and as it were revive the spirits'. It was not enough to admire the flowers: the real enthusiast had to procure them and look after them himself. 'Anemones,' for example, 'are so full of variety and so dainty that the sight of them doth enforce an earnest longing desire in the minde of anyone to be the possessour of some of them at least.' Needlework, like gardening, is a time-consuming activity demanding patience and perseverance; the embroiderer shares the keen plantsman's 'earnest longing desire' to possess certain plants, and in embroidery she has the added satisfaction of prolonging their natural life span.

Anemones in Parkinson's Paradisus Terrestris

A lady inspects her tulips in the 'Spring' section of Crispin de Pass's A Garden of Flowers. Note the variety of flowering bulbs

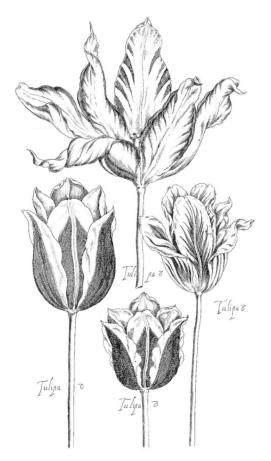

Mid-seventeenth-century tent stitch picture of a musical garden party. Tulips feature in the beds below the balustrade and on the embroidered dress of the lady on the right

Tulips from Le Jardin du Roi showing the distinctive feathered and flamed markings admired by gardeners and embroiderers alike

OUTLANDISH FLOWERS

Among the most covetable flowers were exotic newcomers such as tulips, which Parkinson described as 'Outlandish', to distinguish them from 'English' natives – 'our age being more delighted in the search, curiosity and rarity of these pleasant delights than any age I think before'. Tulipomania in Britain never reached the same heights as in Holland, but the 'wonderful variety and mixture of the colours' and 'their stately and delightfull forme' made tulips among the most costly and highly prized of all 'Outlandish' flowers. It is easy to see how collectors, gardeners and embroiderers must all have been spellbound by these and other bulbous plants – and who could tell what rare properties, strange shapes and wondrous sizes might yet appear? The lady admiring her tulips in the spring garden illustrated in Crispin de Pass's *Hortus Floridus* makes delightfully clear

the pleasure and excitement of collecting and cultivating such novelties. The design of the garden in the engraving has hardly changed since the last century, but the choice collection of plants is far more varied than before, including iris, crocus, hyacinths, narcissi, lilies and, in the place of honour, a crown imperial. In 1615 many of these were recent introductions to Europe. The crown imperial, which grew wild in Persia, had been sent to Vienna by the botanist de l'Ecluse in 1576, and the crocus was a gift to John Gerard from Jean Robin in Paris. Robin was the director of Henri IV's gardens at the Louvre, and of special interest to us because of his connection with the King's embroiderer, Pierre Vallet, who created the designs worked by Marie de Medici and the ladies of her court. Vallet was always looking for new subjects and based many of his designs on the plants he found in Robin's own garden, which was full of novelties and was often visited

by Queen Marie herself. Soon Robin was growing rarities especially for Vallet to engrave as motifs for embroidery. The King became patron of their project, and in 1608 the finest blooms were assembled in a book entitled *Le Jardin du Roi Henri IV*, dedicated in the most extravagant terms to the Queen. Although it was intended as a pattern book the exquisite flowers were treated naturalistically, making them less useful for the embroiderer than those in the latter part of Crispin de Pass's *A Garden of Flowers*, where the plants have been somewhat simplified in outline. His book was originally intended for colouring, but the outlines have equal appeal for the embroiderer; the flower sprigs and clusters of nuts and fruit are transformed into miniature trees set on hillocks inhabited by birds, insects and fictitious plants which add to the decorative and fanciful effect. It is interesting that the copy belonging to Mrs Earle, the well-known Victorian writer on gardens,

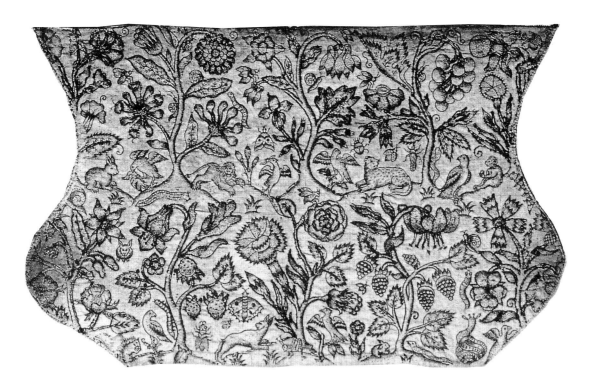

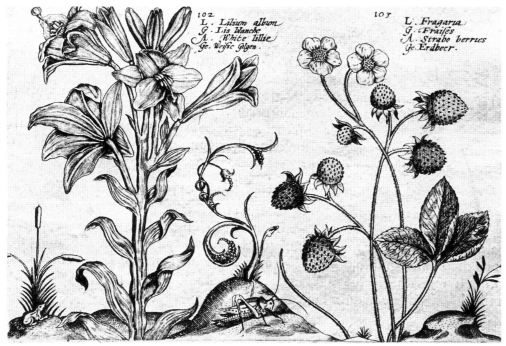

Above *An early seventeenth-century coif or lady's cap printed and partly worked in black silk with small creatures and multi-flowering plants growing from small mounds. The decorative effect resembles the fanciful treatment of plants in* A Garden of Flowers *(below)*

was 'well preserved, though some Philistine lady of the last century has with patient industry pricked some of the flowers and insects all round for the purpose of taking the outlines for patterns'.

In the seventeenth century, the native flowers of Elizabethan embroidery were joined by 'Outlandish' newcomers, some real and some entirely imaginary. These mysterious multi-flowering and fruiting plants appeared on dress and furnishings, and though they seem merely to be figments of the embroiderer's imagination, such wonderful creations were also the ambition of every gardener interested in the secrets of grafting.

THE PLEASANT DELIGHTS OF A CURIOUS ORCHARD

In his *Description of England* of 1587, William Harrison had admired the skill of gardeners who were 'not only excellent in grafting the natural fruits, but also in their artificial mixtures whereby one tree brings forth sundry fruits of divers colours and tastes, dallying with nature in her course, as if her whole trade were perfectly known to them'. Fruit-growing and grafting were of absorbing interest, encouraged by books with titles like *The Fruiterer's Secrets* and *Cornucopia, a Miscellaneum of*

Multi-fruiting tree embroidered in coloured silks in the first part of the seventeenth century. The variety of fruit recalls the contemporary craze for grafting

Below *Grafting practices illustrated in Leonard Meager's* The English Gardener *of 1670*

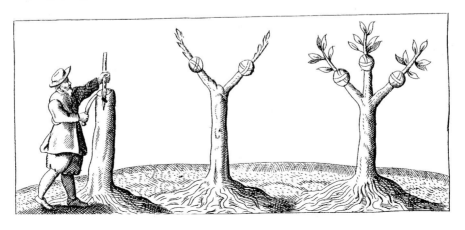

Above *Fruit tree design by Marian Kratochwil based on a long cushion c.1600, in the Victoria & Albert Museum*

Miniature trees laden with fruit and stiff flowers set on shaded rococo stitch hillocks in a mid-seventeenth-century picture

Lucriferous and Most Fructiferous Experiments, full of strange theories and instructions for grafting different fruit on a single plant. Ladies perusing Sir Hugh Platt's *Floraes Paradise* might have paused when, for example, they read his suggestion for 'grafting plummes on a willow to come without stones', and imagined how decorative the effect of such a strange hybrid might be in needlework.

Some embroidered trees bore a variety of fruit, as if the gardener's dreams had at last come true, their wonderful crops reminiscent of Andrew Marvell's poem describing the pleasures of the garden:

> What wond'rous life is this I lead!
> Ripe apples drop about my head;
> The luscious clusters of the vine
> Upon my mouth do crush their Wine;
> The Nectarine and curious Peach
> Into my hands themselves do reach;
> Stumbling on melons, as I pass
> Insnar'd with Flow'rs, I fall on grass.

Seventeenth-century orchards were well stocked with a rich variety of tree and soft fruits, and were designed to be as decorative as the pleasure garden, set out with paths, arbours and fountains. The flower season (which had yet to be extended by plant introductions from China and Japan) was much shorter than today, and the orchard was doubly appreciated for its beauty in autumn. Vineyards and orchards were among the 'Flowers, Starres and Paradises of the Earth' for Ralph Austen, a nurseryman with a gift for poetic prose, who described their delights in *A Treatise of Fruit Trees* in 1653, echoing Gerard's 'robe of imbroidered work': 'Is it not a pleasant sight to behold a multitude of Trees round about, in decent forme and order, bespangled, and gorgeously apparalled with green Leaves, Bloomes and goodly Fruits, as with a rich robe of imbroidered work, or as hanging with some precious Jewels or Pearles, the Boughs laden, and burdened downe to you, and freely offering their ripe fruits, as a large satisfaction of all your labours.'

The orchard was a cornucopia for all the senses, and garden writers like William Coles in *The Art of Simpling* in 1652 described the visual enchantments, the fragrant smells, and even the *feel* of the plants, 'some as soft as silke and some prickly as an Hedgehog ... The eares have their recreation in the pleasant noise of warbling notes, which the chaunting birds accent forth among the

murmuring leaves'. The numerous birds worked in the embroidery of the period are an indication of the seventeenth-century gardener's affection for them. Fruit trees were colourful and decorative, and the embroiderer, attracted by their luscious crops, often exaggerated the size of the fruit on the trees. But was her work quite as fanciful as it appears? Trees on which several varieties are grafted are commonplace now, and so are dwarfing stocks which make picking the fruit a far less tedious business as

well as fitting into smaller gardens. However, they were already a reality in Stuart gardens. Dwarfing stocks had been imported from France since the end of the sixteenth century; they were illustrated in specialist books, and pruning methods to keep the trees small were clearly described in *Floraes Paradise*: 'If you would have an orchard of dwarfe trees, suffering none to grow above a yard high...nippe off all the green buds when they first come forth, which you find in the top of the tree, with your fingers.'

CABINETS OF CURIOSITY

Just such an orchard can be seen inside the cabinet shown below, where ingeniously made miniature fruit trees are set in a four-square plot closely resembling the orchard depicted on the title page of Ralph Austen's *Treatise of Fruit Trees*. The cabinet is a fine example of a technique now commonly referred to as stumpwork, but known to its makers as raised work – a more accurate description of the extraordinary three-dimensional effects achieved by padding and applying detached motifs. It became a craze in the second half of the century, its popularity reflecting the passionate interest of the age in the exotic, the curious and the merely odd, summed up in that real cabinet of

curiosities known as Tradescant's Ark. This was set up in their garden at Lambeth by John Tradescant and his son, two of the greatest gardeners, explorers and collectors of the age. The Ark contained the weirdest miscellany of objects, 'Two Feathers of the Phoenix Tale. Elephants head and tayle only. Flea chains of silver and gold' to name a few. It was all part of the current taste for collecting together and admiring quite unconnected items, which were esteemed for their 'curiosity'. The embroiderer was following this collecting fashion in putting together oddly assorted motifs and applying minute shells, pearls, pieces of mica and coral, and chips of glinting minerals to create wonderfully strange effects in raised work.

A surprisingly large number of cabinets have survived,

Episodes from the story of Abraham ornament the sides of this mid-seventeenth-century raised work box which opens to reveal a miniature orchard. The four-square plan resembles the garden seen on the title page (opposite, below) *of Ralph Austen's* A Treatise of Fruit Trees

Fruit trees and flowers flourish on squares of velvety grass inside the casket. The small statues make ingenious use of ivory knife handles

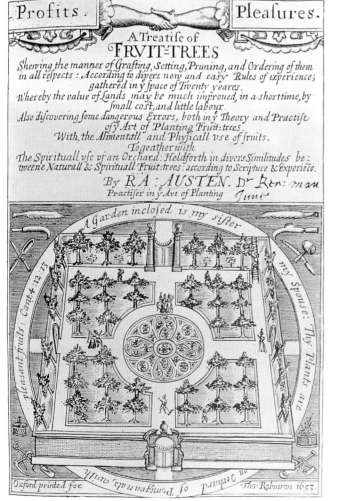

and it is tempting to imagine that John Rea, the author of *Flora*, had them in mind when he wrote in 1665: 'We will proceed to the Flower-Garden, and fashion it in the form of a cabinet with several boxes fit to receive Nature's choicest jewels.' Parkinson, too, had thought of his flowers as precious jewels, and Rea intended his book to describe the new plants that had arrived since Parkinson's day. Again it was the variety of plants that appealed to him. 'A choice collection of living beauties, rare plants, flowers and fruit' were 'indeed the wealth, glory and delight of the garden... and the most absolute indication of the owner's ingenuity, whose skill and care is chiefly required in their choice culture and position.'

The embroiderer chose her flowers and worked them with amazing ingenuity and skill. She placed them in a wonderland setting quite unlike the detailed replicas of gardens depicted in the Elizabethan furnishings – though still peopled by a similar cast of biblical and allegorical characters, now dressed in the fashions worn at the courts of Charles I and Charles II, with laces and periwigs instead of ruffs and farthingales.

By the middle of the century, fashions in great gardens were beginning to reflect the influence of the new French formal gardens – grander, yet simpler and far more unified in style. But English flower-lovers continued either to give their flowers a little plot by themselves, or followed John Rea in making a 'complex fret' of small beds to display their collections. Rea (writing in 1665) emphatically rejected the open and plainer style of the French garden, which he

Left *Plain grass plots herald the new formal style in this illustration from John Worlidge's* Systema Horticulturae

Above *Stumpwork could create three-dimensional effects as fanciful as any seen in topiary. The butterflies, nuts, fruits and flowers in this mid-seventeenth-century picture are worked in a variety of needlelace stitches; the grotto-like pool is encrusted with purl and beads*

called an 'immured nothing'. He preferred 'the essential ornaments, the verdant carpets of many pretty plants and pleasing flowers' with which even a green meadow was 'spontaneously embroidered'. The frontispiece of John Worlidge's *Systema Horticulturae* of 1677 depicts plain grass plots in the new style, but in his engaging text flowers continue to feature in both great and cottage gardens, and for those 'denied the priviledge of having a real garden', he suggests an indoor alternative using 'boxes, pots and other receptacles for Flowers, Plants etc', or the creation of 'curious Representations of Banquets of Fruits, Flower pots, Gardens and such like … painted to the life to please the Eyes and satisfye the fancy of such that either cannot obtain the Felicity of enjoying them in reality, or to supply the defect that Winter annually brings'.

Though Worlidge does not mention them, many of the most curious 'Representations of Flowers and Gardens' were in embroidery, either in canvas work, silk stitchery, stumpwork or beadwork, and they have real and interesting links with contemporary garden literature. The trees, as we have seen, reflect popular grafting and dwarfing practices, and the flowers echo the gardener's ambition to make blooms as vivid, exotic and showy as possible. 'Nature often times lyketh to play with…Flowers,' wrote Parkinson, producing double blooms and sports like the 'fruitful or much-bearing marigold…likewise called Jackanapes on horseback', and the embroiderer, working silk-covered stems and minute, brilliantly coloured, streaked and spotted petals in needlelace, could join in the game, creating raised work flowers as 'rare and faire' as any admired in the garden.

VERDANT SCULPTURE

The amusement of stumpwork – both to execute and to look at – has an affinity with the pleasures of topiary, which continued in vogue well into the next century. The craze for clipping plants into fanciful shapes was already well advanced in the sixteenth century. In 1577 Barnaby Goodge had recommended that rosemary could be 'sette by women for their pleasure to growe in sundry proportions as in the fashion of a Cart, a Peacock, or such like things as they fancie'. Parkinson favoured yew, because no other plant was so apt 'to be cut, lead or drawne into what forme you will, whether of beasts, birds or men'. Lord Bacon, however, considered topiary figures 'cut out in juniper' childish, though paradoxically he did like the idea of having fruit grown into moulds to provide amusing items for dessert so 'you may have apples in the form of pears or lemons', or even 'figures of men, beasts or birds'

Beadwork basket, c.1675, said to have been made by the 20-year-old Elizabeth Clarke (1655–99), lavishly adorned with three-dimensional lemons, acorns, flowers and leaves. The couple in the fruit arbour are worked on satin

Topiary introduces a note of humour to the garden and is as much fun to stitch as it is to fashion in evergreens. Here Belinda Downes visualizes Pope's topiary 'Queen Elizabeth' and 'St George and the Dragon' as stumpwork, and devises a border pattern inspired by contemporary engravings of topiary

– confections as curious as any contrived by embroiderers! Indeed the quaint but charming company assembled on the embroiderer's ground with their strange shapes and peculiar discrepancies of scale was mirrored in the real garden by the verdant shapes of 'dogs, bulls, fishes and fowl', made by patient training of evergreens over frames, as suggested by Sir Hugh Platt in *The Garden of Eden* or Gervase Markham in *The Countrie Farme*.

Topiary came to have its detractors, however. In his essay on 'Verdant Sculpture', published in *The Guardian* in 1713, Alexander Pope attacked the excesses of the topiary fashion, and his celebrated 'Catalogue of Greens' lists items as whimsical as any to be found in stumpwork. They include:

Adam and Eve in Yew, Adam a little shatter'd by the fall of the Tree of Knowledge in the great Storm: Eve and the Serpent very flourishing…

St George in Box: his Arm scarce long enough, but will be in Condition to stick the Dragon by next April.

A green Dragon of the same, with a Tail of Ground-Ivy for the present. N.B. These two not to be Sold separately.

Edward the Black Prince in Cypress.

A Laurustine bear in blossom with a juniper hunter in berries.

A Pair of Giants, stunted, to be sold cheap.

A Queen Elizabeth in Phylyraea (*Phillyrea* is a small-leaved evergreen), a little inclining to the Green Sickness but full of growth…

Divers eminent Modern Poets in Bays, somewhat blighted, to be disposed of a Pennyworth.

A Quickset Hog shot up into a Porcupine, by being forgot a Week in rainy Weather.

A Lavender Pig, with Sage growing in his Belly.

Noah's ark in holly, standing on the mount, the ribs a little damaged for want of water.

Bear-baiting – a mid-seventeenth-century suggestion for topiary

SHADES OF ALICE

Although Lord Bacon did not care for topiary, a number of the garden features he did approve of sound just as fanciful as those found in Stuart needlework. His imaginary garden was to be laid out formally on 12 hectares (30 acres) of ground with a succession of flowers for each month, but the main garden was not to be 'too busie, or full of Work'. 'Knots of figures, with divers coloured earths' aroused the same displeasure as topiary: 'they be but Toyes: You may see as good Sights, many times, in Tarts' (Bacon was here referring to the elaborately decorated tarts made for banquets and filled with colourful jellies and preserves. Skill at preserving and presenting food were accomplishments on a par with gardening and needlework). A third of the garden was to be informally and prettily planted as 'a natural wilderness' with the grass powdered with flowers and strawberries. Here there were to be 'little heaps in the nature of mole hills...to be set some with wild thyme; some with pinks; some with germander; some with strawberries' – and topped by nicely pruned standards – roses, evergreens and fruit such as redcurrants. Lord Bacon's essays were so well known that many embroiderers were likely to have read them, and some would surely have detected a resemblance between his description and their own embroidered scenes, where people, fruit trees, buildings, flowers and animals were often set on small mounds, or among undulating hillocks receding gently into the background, both mounds and hillocks acting as useful devices for isolating one incident or character from another.

In one such embroidery, a striking lily stands on the far side of a pool, between a gentleman and a lady who holds a posy of flowers, reminding me of the (much later) scene in *Alice through the Looking Glass* in which Alice endeavoured to climb the hill in order to see into the garden. She wandered among corkscrew paths until finally she came upon a large flowerbed. 'Oh Tiger Lily!' said Alice, addressing herself to one that was waving gracefully about in the wind, 'I *wish* you could talk!' 'We *can* talk,' said the Tiger Lily, 'when there's anybody worth talking to.'

The scale and atmosphere in Stuart embroidery make such a conversation seem quite possible. 'Into your garden you can walk,' suggested John Rea in *Flora*, 'and with each plant and flower talk', and although Stuart embroiderers could not enjoy Lewis Carroll's fantasies, they might have come across Ralph Austen's *Dialogue, or familiar discourse between the Husbandman and Fruit Trees* published in 1676. The husbandman walking in an orchard asks the fruit trees if they really can talk, to which they reply that they can, and in 'all languages' too. In the needlework scenes of the period the tops of the trees are on just the right level to speak to the people around them; and indeed the peculiarities of scale put plants, animals, people and insects all on the same footing. In these embroideries the bizarre is translated into visual terms, capturing the atmosphere of strangeness so apparent in the poetry of

A large lily and upright caterpillar are among the disproportionate motifs on this tent stitch cushion made to support an open bible or prayer book

Beehives in an early seventeenth-century flower garden

Andrew Marvell. In the poem 'Upon Appleton House', Marvell wrote: 'Men like Grasshoppers appear/ But Grasshoppers are Gyants there'; and in 'The Garden' he describes a knot laid out as an elaborate sundial, a target for bees and insects:

> And, as it works the industrious Bee
> Computes its time as well as we.
> How could such sweet and wholesome Hours
> Be reckon'd but with herbes and flow'rs.

The bee is like Spenser's butterfly (see page 37), and the quantity of insects in Elizabethan and Stuart embroidery reflects both the scientific interest and the affection they inspired at the time – especially bees, which, like plants, had virtues and properties. 'Bees are kept throughout the world for the delicate Food, pleasant Drink and wholesome Physic they yield,' wrote John Worlidge in 1677, praising their industry, intelligence and 'curious architecture'. In July 1654, the diarist John Evelyn had a transparent beehive given him by the 'most obliging and universally curious Dr Wilkins' of Wadham College, Oxford, who had transparent apiaries 'built like castles and palaces' so that he might study the habits of the bees. Entire books were written about them and one, *The Feminine Monarchie* written by Charles Butler in 1623, even included a bees' madrigal with the notes hummed by the Queen and her workers written out in staves. The embroidered insects match these rather fey notions to perfection, for the tiny creatures seem to have personalities of their own, like the intimate and friendly flowers, animals and people around them.

SILVER FOUNTAINS

In Shakespeare's sonnet XXXI, 'Roses have thorns and silver fountains mud,/ Clouds and eclipses stain both moon and sun/ And loathsome canker lies in sweetest bud'. In the embroidered garden, though, the smiling sun always shines, the flowers are in full bloom, and the fountains and pools are clear and glittering. They appear in countless stumpwork and tent stitch scenes depicting David and Bathsheba or Susannah and the Elders, and for the embroiderer they were as much an opportunity for a virtuoso performance as they were in real gardens, so popular that they were frequently included whether a part of the story or not. Shapes, colours and textures were combined and contrasted, using all the stitches and materials at the embroiderer's command. The water could be patterned horizontally and the surrounding rocks vertically, and tiny spirals of purl (coils of painted or silk-covered wire), beads and spangles glinted among them just as the minerals did in the real watery grottoes of the time.

Possibly the most famous water feature was at Enstone in Oxfordshire. This was constructed round a real rock, as jagged and curious in outline as any devised by the embroiderer. The rock was enclosed in a building and was the central feature in a spectacular water display mounted for guests after they had banqueted in the upper room. Here the ceiling repeated the watery theme with paintings

Opposite *Joke fountains were favourite garden features, more amusing for hosts than guests. Those at Enstone, illustrated in Plot's* Natural History of Oxfordshire, *soaked visitors to the grotto with spouts, 'hedges' and canopies of water*

Above *In this mid-seventeenth-century stumpwork picture Bathsheba dabbles her feet in a small brick-built pool. The naughty look in the fountain figure's eye suggests the possibility of a water-joke, as (right) in the 'Statue of a Woman, that at the turning of a private Cock, shall cast Water out of her Nipples into the Spectators Faces' in Worlidge's* Systema Horticulturae *(1677)*

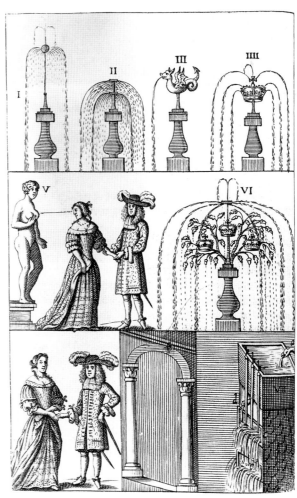

of Susannah and the Elders and Hagar finding the well. The rock and the room around it concealed a network of pipes controlled by cocks to produce spellbinding effects. A great jet of water tossed up a silver ball and arcs of falling water seen through the sunlight created an artificial rainbow.

These ingenious waterworks originally came from the gardens of Renaissance Italy, together with joke fountains which gave visitors a 'thorough wetting' when they were installed in great English gardens like Hampton Court, Theobalds and Whitehall. In John Worlidge's book *Systema Horticulturae* the illustration of various fountains is equally humorous and lighthearted, and his remarks on grottoes seem as appropriate for the embroiderer as for the gardener. 'It is a place that is capable of giving you so much pleasure and delight that you may bestow not undeservedly what

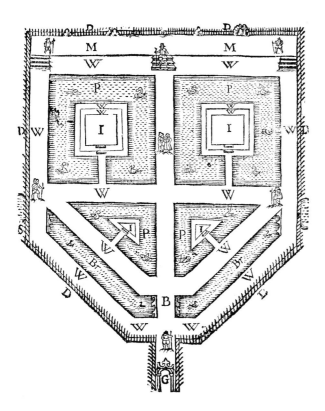

cost you may please on it, by paving it with marble or immuring it with stone or Rockwork, either naturally or resembling the excellencies of Nature.'

Fountains were often set in fish ponds which were both ornamental and useful. In August 1685 John Evelyn visited Lady Clarendon's house at Swallowfield in Berkshire, where he admired the 'delicious and rarest fruits' in the orchard, and the fine trees, shrubs and flowers – 'My lady being so extraordinarily skill'd in the flowery part, and my lord in diligence of planting... but above all, the canall and fish ponds, fed by a quick and swift river, so well and plentifully stor'd with fish that for pike, carp, breame and tench I never saw anything approaching it'. Over 30 years before, Evelyn had made his own triangular fish ponds with an 'artificial rock' next to the 'little retiring place' he built in the meadow at Wooton in Surrey and there are also plans for triangular fish ponds in Gervase Markham's *A Way to get Wealth*, published in 1638. There were special mounts above the ponds where one might enjoy the sight of the fish as they 'show to the sun their wav'd coats dropt with gold'. This phrase, from Milton's *Paradise Lost*, seems equally apt to describe the embroidered fish leaping in the rocky pools beneath the gold-rayed sun. Their bodies gleam with metal threads and pieces of purl, waved and chequered with tiny patterns ingeniously worked out to contrast with the stitchery of the water and the plumage of the birds which float among them – ducks, swans and kingfishers – as well as the occasional mermaid, complete with comb, mirror and elegant tail.

The embroiderers' creations share the fanciful quality of the artificial fish ornamenting the bed of the stream at Hatfield. Set among gorgeous shells and mysterious rocks, they were made lifelike by the reflections of the water pouring into the stream from an extraordinary marble basin dominated by a statue of Neptune standing on painted artificial rocks. Even closer to the artifice of the needlework ponds and rocks was Francis Bacon's water garden at Gorhambury, where there was a lake with flowery islands presided over by statues of nymphs and tritons. Round the lake were gilt images and 'glasses coloured for the eye', and the bottom of the lake was covered with pebbles of several colours which were 'worked into various figures such as fish'. In the imaginary garden of his essay, Bacon recommended similar glittering effects. The surface of the pond or pool was to be 'embellished with coloured glass and such things of lustre'. The two types of fountain he described can both be seen in contemporary embroidered gardens: 'the one, that sprinkleth or spouteth water; the other a fair receipt of water of some thirty or forty

Opposite *'A platform for ponds' from Gervase Markham's* A Way to get Wealth *of 1638. The walks between the ponds were to be ornamented with fruit trees, and mounts were to be set up in the corners*

A fountain plays into a grotto-like fish pond embellished with beads and coral in this raised work garden scene made in the second half of the seventeenth century

foot square but without fish or slime or mud'. The second kind 'which we may call a bathing pool' is reduced to the dimensions of a plunging pool by the embroiderer. Such pools did exist – like the one at Packwood House in Warwickshire, still complete with its brick walls – just as they appear in the embroidered scenes.

At Hatfield, Robert Cecil employed French experts to create the wonderful water garden, and John Tradescant, his gardener, supplied shells for the stream. The garden contained twenty-four figures of golden lions – harking back to Cardinal Wolsey's day, when the Pond Garden at Hampton Court boasted scores of carved and gilded 'heraldic' beasts. These creatures were also seen in the knots and topiary, 'made all of herbs of dulcet sweetness'.

In the seventeenth century there were real menageries and aviaries where rare animals and birds were on view.

James I had established a menagerie in St James's Park, much enlarged by Charles II, who introduced the famous pelicans and the improbable figure of a crane with a wooden leg. Wild beasts were a part of the embroidered gardens too. Lions with manes as meticulously curled and waved as a gentleman's periwig sit smiling on grassy hummocks, or stand twirling their tails opposite spotted leopards, both equally uninterested in the sheep, stags, unicorns and camels on the surrounding slopes. The embroiderer chose these wild and mythical animals to inhabit the garden from the patterns then available in books. Whether she was aware of it or not, she was following a tradition that goes back to the menageries attached to royal palaces, like the one at Woodstock in Oxfordshire where Henry I kept 'lyons, leopards and strange spotted beasts, porcupines, camells and such like animals'.

CHAPTER 3

The Grand Manner

'This garden, as a Pattern, may be shown
To those who would add Beauty to their own'
RENÉ RAPIN, *OF GARDENS*, 1666, TRANSLATED BY JOHN EVELYN THE YOUNGER, 1673

PARTERRES OF EMBROIDERY

The pattern of gardens in the 1660s differed dramatically from those of the previous century, and 'those who would add Beauty to their own' now found their inspiration in the impressive large-scale designs of the French formal style – the Grand Manner – which Charles II had admired during his exile at the court of his cousin Louis XIV. On his return to England at the Restoration in 1660 he adopted the French style, transforming the appearance of Hampton Court and St James's Park with long vistas, avenues and straight canals. The 'delightful confusion' of flowers and patterns in the compartments of the Elizabethan garden had no place in these spacious designs, and little by little the knots gave way to unified composi-tions of beds known as parterres, varying in complexity from geometric grass plots which were sometimes edged with narrow flower borders known as *parterres à l'Angloise*, or, 'in the English Manner', to elaborate box scrollwork resembling embroidery set out on a ground of sand or coloured earth, appropriately named *parterres de broderie*.

The simplest kind of English parterre with plain grass plots flanked by neatly clipped rows of trees is charmingly recorded in a picture of Queen Esther kneeling before King Ahasuerus that was worked early in the eighteenth century. In Elizabethan days each bed in the four-square plot would have been patterned or planted differently, but now it is symmetry rather than variety that is all important, seen to most striking effect in the parterres of embroidery where the scrollwork patterns planted in box echoed the exuberant designs embroidered on fashionable dress.

The similarity was remarkable, as George London, one of the foremost nurserymen and designers in the reigns of William and Mary and Queen Anne, pointed out in *The Retir'd Gardener* of 1710 when he endeavoured to explain to British gardeners exactly what was meant by the term *parterre de broderie*. 'Imbroidery,' he wrote, 'is those Draughts which represent in Effect those we have on our Cloaths, and that look like foliage, and these Sorts of Figures in Gardener's language are called *Branchwork*. Below this certain flowers seem to be drawn which is the part of the Imbroidery which we call *Flourishings*.'

The use of the word 'embroidery' as a gardening term is here far more explicit than in the poetic comparisons of John Gerard's and Ralph Austen's 'robes of imbroidered work'. It recurs frequently in contemporary manuals, and in his *Garden Book* of 1653 Sir Thomas Hanmer, a noted flower enthusiast with a superb garden in Flintshire, found it useful when describing the transition from the old style to the Grand Manner. 'The whole designs or laying out of garden grounds are much different to what our fathers

Opposite, above *Early eighteenth-century tent stitch picture of Esther before Ahasuerus, based on an illustration* (below left) *in Gerard De Jode's* Historiae Sacrae Veteris et Novi Testamenti, *a favourite source of embroidery designs. The pattern-drawer has altered the illustration,* *replacing the gruesome scene of the hanging of Mordecai with a vignette of a house and walled garden laid out as a* parterre à l'Angloise. *An equally symmetrical but grander version of this type of parterre with statues and plants in pots is illustrated in John Worlidge's* Systema Horticulturae (below right)

used,' he wrote. 'In these days the borders are not hedged about with privet, rosemary or other such herbs which hide the view and prospect…all is now commonly near the house laid open and exposed to the sight of the rooms and chambers…If the ground be spacious, the next adjacent quarters or parterres, as the French call them, are of fine turf, but as low as any green to bowl on; cut out curiously into embroidery of flowers and shapes of arabesques, animals and birds, or feuillages [leaf shapes], and the small alleys or intervals filled with several coloured sands and dust with much art, with but few flowers in such knots, and those only such as grow very low, lest they spoil the beauty of the embroidery.' Intricate knot patterns were still appearing in garden manuals when Sir Thomas wrote this, so it is no surprise to find him confusing the terms knot and parterre. As in the open knots, the patterns showed to the best advantage when laid out on a ground of sand, gravel or coloured earth – brick and coal dust were both used – which contrasted with the green of the box.

The elegant effect can be seen in the parterre of embroidery worked on a fire screen at Packwood House (see page 68) where the four matching quarters of the design frame an eye-catching sea-horse fountain. The pattern would look most striking seen from the house or from the balustraded terrace, and in a picture worked early in the eighteenth century the embroiderer, Elizabeth Haines (see page 69), stitched her initials below the central window of the first floor as if to indicate that this was the best viewpoint for admiring the parterre. Her choice of colours suggests that the matching motifs were laid out in double rows of low clipped box enclosing narrow bands and circles of white sand with the spaces filled in with yellow gravel. This scheme makes a pleasing contrast with the paler green of the turf – 'the different colours serving to set off the Parterre the better'. This was how George London described the effect, and in his terms Elizabeth Haines' parterre was 'composed of Imbroidery and grass plots which look very well in little gardens as well as in great'.

The term *parterre de broderie* was already in use early in the seventeenth century when Claude Mollet was laying out embroidery-like designs in box for Henry IV in his gardens at Saint Germain-en-Laye and Fontainebleau. Mollet's son André, also an expert gardener, worked in England for Charles I, and in 1670 his book of plans for gardens, parterres and labyrinths, *The Pleasure Garden*, was translated into English, providing British enthusiasts with a whole variety of handsome designs. The embroidery parterres reached their zenith in the gardens of Louis XIV at Vaux-le-Vicomte and Versailles, but the fashion for them continued all over Europe well into the eighteenth century. As late as the 1780s, William Beckford, creator of Fonthill Abbey and gardens, travelling in Holland saw 'stiff parterres scrawled and flourished like the embroidery of an old maid's work bag'. He may have been

thinking of the effect embroiderers created with threads knotted using a special shuttle and then couched down in patterns as elaborate and formal as a real *parterre de broderie*.

In England the most spectacular embroidery parterres were to be seen in the semicircular layout of the Great Fountain Garden at Hampton Court, designed by Daniel Marot for William and Mary and completed in 1689. Looking down on the designs from the first-floor apartments of Sir Christopher Wren's new building, Queen Mary may well have been reminded of the patterns of

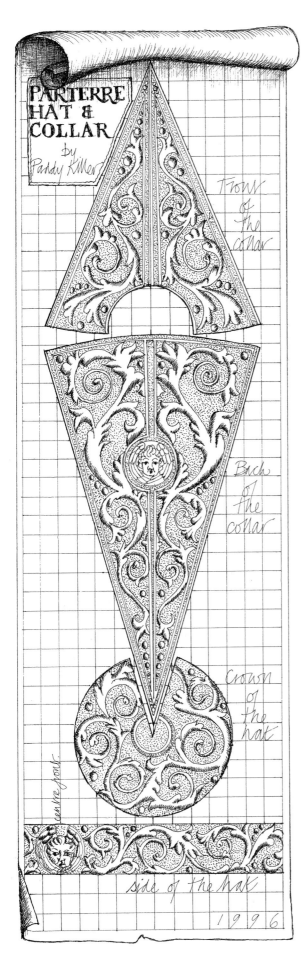

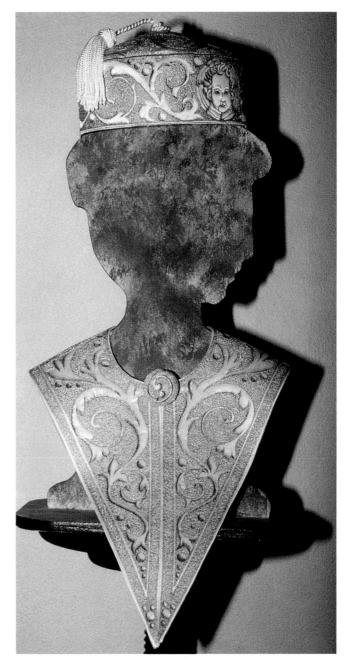

Opposite, above 'Parterres of Embroidery are so called because the Box wherewith they are planted, imitates Embroidery upon the Ground', wrote John James in The Theory and Practice of Gardening (1712). A parterre in box scrollwork from Pluche's Spectacle de La Nature, 1740, 'imitates' the edge-to-edge effect of an early eighteenth-century gentleman's waistcoat (below) worked in silver-gilt thread.

Above The free-flowing patterns of the parterre designs can be effectively updated for contemporary dress, as Paddy Killer demonstrates in this hat and collar machine-quilted on satin. Her design for the embroidery, drawn in the manner of a garden plan, is shown left

The symmetrical patterns of the embroidery parterre complement the regular design of the house in this early eighteenth-century tent stitch pole screen. Following the Dutch fashion popularized by William and Mary, evergreens in ornamental pots are set out on pedestals on the terrace and on the parterre; bays, myrtles, phillyrea and citrus fruits could be purchased ready-trimmed to shape at the nurseries of London and Wise at Brompton in South Kensington. Similar parterres (left) were illustrated in The Retir'd Gardener

The parterres of embroidery were designed to be seen from one direction, and the endearingly naïve perspective of Elizabeth Haines' garden (left) *underlines the axial emphasis of the design with its broad central walk and steps up to the terrace. Beyond the gate she embellished the grass with large striped carnations and tulips. Though flowers were sometimes grown in narrow borders edging the parterres, they were excluded from the 'Imbroidery' which worked best in low uniform lines of box; but, as Sir Thomas Hanmer noted in his* Garden Book, *the florists (enthusiasts for a group of particularly decorative flowers) could always cultivate their treasures in 'a little private seminary' somewhere else in the garden.*

The importance of viewing the parterre from above is shown in a late eighteenth-century engraving of the gardens at La Muette (above); the beauty of the pattern is lost when seen from this angle

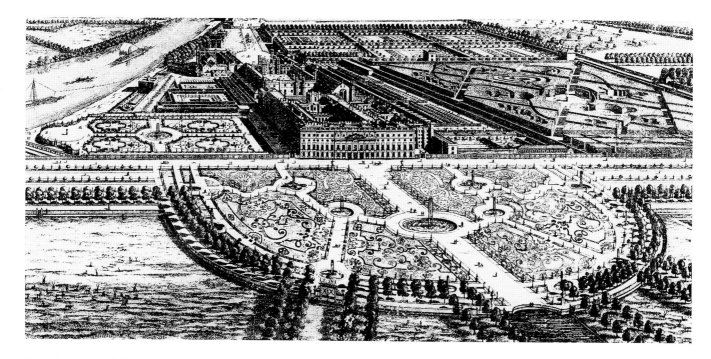

knotting, one of the methods of needlework she is known to have enjoyed. She shared her husband's delight in gardening, and just as his enthusiasm for it made gentlemen follow 'everwhere, with such a gust [gusto] that the alteration is indeed wonderful throughout the whole kingdom', so her love of needlework made it 'as much the fashion to work [i.e. stitch], as it had been formerly to be idle'. Celia Fiennes, whose *Journeys* record her travels round England in the reign of William and Mary, saw the work of Queen Mary and her ladies furnishing an entire closet at Hampton Court, executed in satin stitch in worsteds. This was most probably crewelwork, which was in vogue throughout Mary's reign, its exuberant swirling designs, like those of knotting and of the Indian chintzes she collected, echoing the sweeping curves of box scrollwork in the embroidery parterres nearest the palace.

The patterns of crewelwork were freer than the exactly matched designs of the parterres, but their general effect was equally bold and vigorous. For the embroiderer they were a welcome change from the exquisite minuteness of blackwork and the precision of canvaswork and stumpwork, yet she could still show off her inventiveness in the patterning of leaves, flowers and birds. Early in the seventeenth century, crewelwork on both dress and furnishings repeated the patterns and coiling stems of blackwork, but by the middle of the century the luxuriant foliage was arranged in far more dynamic designs on hangings which filled the high-ceilinged rooms with swirling leaves and stems, creating yet another form of the perennial 'garden within doors'. Once again the hangings would outlast living decorations like those suggested in the 1675 edition of Sir Hugh Plant's *The Garden of Eden*. He proposed that vines should be let in through a window pane and trained all over the room for summer enjoyment.

The effect of a 'garden within doors', even fresher and

Knyff's bird's-eye view of Hampton Court c.1690 shows the swirling patterns of box embroidery framed in English parterres in the Great Fountain Garden. The exuberant designs resemble those worked in knotting and crewelwork. The Privy Garden can be seen on the left

A panel of knotting in thick brown thread

more fanciful than the crewelwork hangings, might also have been created using the bright painted chintzes imported by the East India Company. In 1669 the directors noted the 'great practize for printing large branches for hangings', and they began to send out designs similar to the crewelwork branches of stylized oak leaves for the Indian cotton painters to copy. The French traveller

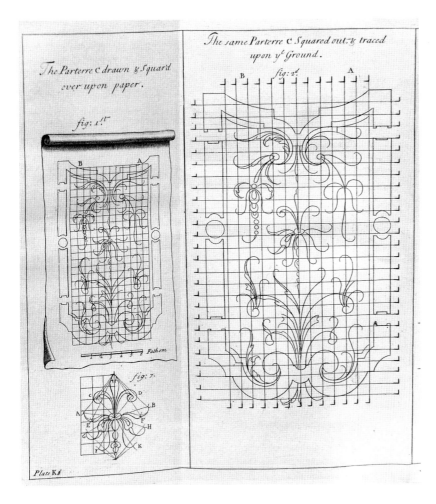

A parterre design from John James' The Theory and Practice of Gardening similar in character to the knotting (opposite) showing how to enlarge the pattern and transfer it to the ground. Embroiderers use exactly the same method. A similar parterre is shown in the frontispiece of The Clergyman's Recreation of 1714 (below left)

Detail of a crewelwork hanging with leaves and stems curving as exuberantly as the 'branchwork and flourishings' of the parterre

The chinoiserie pavilions and plant pots strike an exotic note in this tent stitch picture of a formal garden laid out as an embroidery parterre

François Bernier saw similar hangings when he visited India in the 1660s. He was entertained at Delhi by the Great Mughal in his tent which was 'lined with Masulipatan chintzes figured expressly for that very purpose with flowers so natural and colours so vivid that the tent seemed to be encompassed with real parterres'. Many of the flowers would have seemed intriguingly strange to European eyes. The Indian cotton painters were quite unfamiliar with oak leaves and other Western plants and flowers which they found as outlandish as Parkinson's Scythian lamb. Odd distortions took place in the copying, resulting in hybrids even stranger than the real plants newly introduced to Europe, and these were seized on by the embroiderer as beguiling novelties for exotic garden scenes.

Bernier does not specify which type of parterre the chintzes reminded him of, but their flowery appearance suggests that they were either of 'cutwork' with flowers in *plates bandes* – narrow mounded-up borders laid out to form the pattern – or *à l'Angloise*, grass plots outlined with flower borders. London and his partner Henry Wise listed eleven different kinds of parterre in *The Retir'd Gardener* – small wonder that gardeners then (and now) found the subject confusing! In large gardens several different types of parterre could be combined in a carefully integrated design, but in smaller gardens like Elizabeth Haines', a single parterre aligned on the house was sufficient.

THE STOKE EDITH HANGINGS

Paintings and engravings, especially bird's-eye views, show the impressive scale of gardens in the French formal style with parterres round the house and canals and avenues stretching into the far distance, but it is in needlework that their more intimate, everyday qualities are revealed – indeed the Grand Manner comes most

vividly to life in the pair of large embroidered scenes named after Stoke Edith in Herefordshire where they hung in the Green Velvet Room until the house was destroyed by fire in 1927 (they are now displayed at Montacute House in Somerset). Worked early in the eighteenth century to professionally drawn out designs, they depict the formal garden as an elegant setting for pleasantly leisured lives, and show exactly how it was arranged and planted.

Here we can see just how the grass plots edged with ribbon-like borders of the *parterres à l'Angloise* were

The Stoke Edith orangery hanging records the vogue for 'Greens' and 'Exoticks' in gardens in the Grand Manner. William III thought of evergreens as 'the greatest addition to the beauty of a garden, preserving the figure of a place, even in the roughest part of an inclement and tempestuous winter', and the embroidery demonstrates

the highly sophisticated effect achieved by contrasting their varied textures, shapes and tones. The colour combinations of striped, feathered and flamed tulips were rendered with similar accuracy, recording the current favourites. Wrought-iron gates were another fashionable feature recorded in needlework

Badeslade's view of Frognall in Kent depicts a typical design in the Grand Manner, with ornamental gardens on two sides of the house. These feature parterres à l'Angloise *remarkably similar to those in the Stoke Edith hangings, and show how the embroidered scenes may have been related to the house. To the far right is an orangery at the end of a long terraced garden with a circular fountain pool aligned on the house, and on the left is a walled enclosure with espaliered fruit and parterres on two levels. Such a layout would explain the different direction of the shadows cast by the topiary in the two needlework gardens*

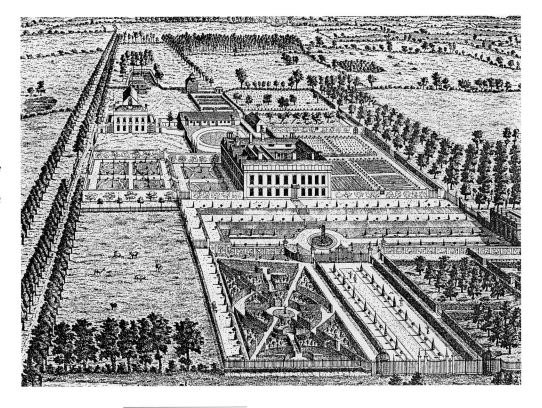

The smaller of the Stoke Edith hangings shows the parterre à l'Angloise *at its most delightful, with spacious gravel paths and grass plots edged with tulips, carnations and clipped evergreens. French gardeners particularly admired the beauty of fine British turf scythed and rolled to velvet smoothness. André Mollet recommended a mix of grasses and herbs like camomile, and this might explain why the embroiderer chose many shades of green to render the subtle effect. The statues, fountain jets and topiary provide vertical interest and enliven the scene. The cupids and fountains are reminiscent of those at Melbourne in Derbyshire, where the Dutch sculptor Van Nost supplied a set of equally exuberant 'boys'*

Above Daniel Marot *illustrates the difference between the various kinds of parterre in his* Nouveau Livre de Parterres *of 1703. Above, unrolled like a carpet, is a* parterre de pièces coupées pour les fleurs, *while below are patterns for parterres of embroidery and English parterres. The latter are grass plots edged with narrow flower borders and punctuated with topiary shapes which cast dark shadows just as they do in the Stoke Edith hangings.*

intended to look, with the bright flowers and varying greens of the shrubs making a subtle contrast of colour and texture to the velvety turf. The dark conical yews standing sentinel at the corners emphasize the symmetry of the design, as do the pairs of statues in both hangings and the fountain pools in the smaller of the two.

Both scenes are viewed from a balustraded terrace so the spectator looks out over the parterres to an orangery in the larger hanging and a semicircular summerhouse with a domed roof in the smaller, beyond which trees and blue-shaded hills are visible. It is tempting to imagine that these are the Malvern Hills which were not far distant from Stoke Edith, and that the hangings show us the gardens Celia Fiennes saw when she visited the house twice in the 1690s. She notes that the gardens are newly 'staked out' and remarks on a summer house and a 'terrace of stone pavements with steps in the middle leading to the garden', and another garden which 'looks towards Herriford town'. On a third visit early in the eighteenth century she mentions a 'fountaine bason' and 'walled gardens and walks one below another'. The embroidered scenes may be purely imaginary, but they do include these features, and perhaps show the completion of the 'staked out' plan. Large-scale furnishing schemes undertaken by the ladies

of the house were not uncommon at the time, and to record one's own garden in the making would have been an engrossing project. The colourful confusion of the seasons, with the fruit ripe on the rosy brick walls while the tulips and carnations are both in full flower, suggests that this might have been the case. The inclusion of the family's pets, the people taking a stroll or enjoying refreshments and the humorous incident of someone tripping on the steps, pursued by a barking spaniel, also strike a highly personal note.

Beautifully trained fruit were a feature in many gardens at the time. One of the finest collections was cultivated by Sir William Temple, the celebrated diplomat who had retired to Moor Park near Farnham in Surrey in 1685 and settled down to enjoy serious garden-making. In his essay *On the Gardens of Epicurus: or of Gardening in the year 1685* (published in 1692) he discusses the perfect garden and speaks admiringly of the Hertfordshire garden belonging to his friend the Countess of Bedford which, like his own, had much in common with the Stoke Edith hangings. Both embroidered scenes are laid out exactly in accordance with his ideal: 'In every garden,' he wrote, 'four things are necessary to be provided for, flowers, fruit, shade and water... The part of your garden next to your house should be a parterre of flowers, or grass plots bordered with

Fan training of fruit trees and vines explained in S. Collin's Paradise Retrieved, 1717. *The branching vine stems create couched patterns against the wall*

flowers.' We may imagine that the needlework gardens lay 'to the best parts of the house... so as to be,' as he put it, 'but like one of the rooms out of which you step into another'. Certainly the embroideries preserve the intimate appeal of a 'garden room', with charming places to sit or walk in shade or sun.

Elegant summerhouses had replaced the leafy arbours of former days because, as John Worlidge wrote, the latter were damp and draughty and 'on a hot day it is pleasanter to sit under a lime tree than to be hoodwinked in an arbour'. Worlidge suggested siting the garden house 'at some remote angle of your garden: For the more remote it is from your house the more private it will be from the frequent disturbances of your Family and friends'. The Stoke Edith summerhouse is also reminiscent of the 'handsome octangular somer-house' described by John Rea in his *Flora*, which was not only a delectable place to sit, but also an ideal spot for useful activities such as sorting out the tulip varieties after the flowering display when the bulbs were 'taken up upon papers, with the names upon them untill they be dried' so that they could be safely stored away in boxes for the next season.

Tulips, especially the flamboyant striped varieties, were still much in vogue, and the hangings show how a prized

Opposite and right *Parterre patterns from* The Theory and Practice of Gardening: far left 'A Parterre of Embroidery of a very new Design', left 'A Parterre of Cut-work for Flowers' *and* right 'A large Parterre of Compartiments'. *The designs might be adapted for appliqué, inlay or shadow work; the speckling and cross hatching are highly suggestive of stitchery*

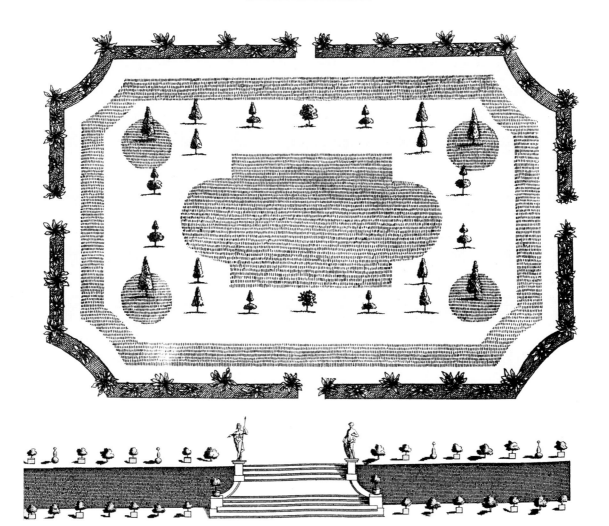

Above *A Bowling Green ornamented with 'little bushes of evergreens' from* The Solitary or Carthusian Gardener, 1706. Bottom right and centre *A Parterre of Orange Trees and rows of clipped evergreens from* The Theory and Practice of Gardening. Bottom left *Orange trees and clipped evergreens decoratively arranged in The Orange Garden at Enghien*

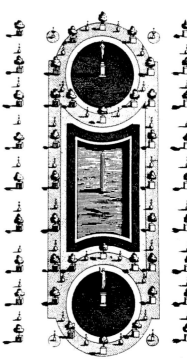

collection was displayed, with a dramatic line-up of individual beauties, so skilfully and accurately rendered that the names of contemporary favourites could be given to many of them. If ideas were needed for authentic spring schemes in the recently restored Privy Garden at Hampton Court or the parterres at Het Loo, William and Mary's splendid garden near Apeldoorn in Holland, the hangings could provide fascinating evidence of contemporary planting, the problem being to find sufficient striped, streaked and feathered varieties to create such a varied display.

Flowers never really lost their appeal to English gardeners, who compromised with the absolute formality of the French style and adapted it to suit their taste, incorporating decorative features such as topiary and 'Exoticks' introduced from Holland by William and Mary. In *Campania Foelix: or Rural Delights*, published in 1700, Timothy Nourse remarked on the importance of having flowers in the borders through the seasons. Seeing a garden without flowers was like sitting down to a meal with the table 'furnisht with Cloth, Plates and Napkins, and nothing serv'd in...' As well as flowers he suggested 'little Bushes of Ever-Greens' spaced evenly all through the borders which would 'look prettily in winter', and so would 'little Firr-Trees', like the ones spaced evenly on the outer borders of the orangery hanging. These could be spruce firs, whose feathery foliage, clipped in tiers, contrasts prettily with the denser effect of juniper, dark yew and variegated holly cut in cones, pyramids and globes. The skilful rendering of individual spiky leaves in the gold and silver hollies suggests that whoever worked them could refer to living models, and the same applies to the orange trees which were worked separately as 'slips' in long armed cross stitch and then applied to the ground, creating yet another sophisticated variation in texture.

Oranges had been grown in England since the sixteenth century, but they were still a rare treat in 1666 when Pepys 'pulled off a little one by stealth' and ate it in Lord Brooke's garden in Hackney. They were among the most admired 'Exoticks', tender plants overwintered in the new greenhouses and orangeries and then set out in carefully chosen containers for an enchantingly decorative summer display. In the Stoke Edith hangings, oranges, lemons and hollies in superb Chinese pots and pretty two-handled vases are arranged in pairs emphasizing the symmetry of the design. Collecting and cultivating 'Exoticks' had become a craze led by Queen Mary, whose glass cases and stoves at Hampton Court housed a spectacular range of plants. In the Stoke Edith orangery hanging special plants are lined up on a grassy slope in front of a row of expertly clipped trees, beyond which we glimpse a sheet of blue, a canal balancing the one embroidered on the extreme right with its pair of gliding swans.

Water played a vital role in the formal gardens. Fountains animated the scene with their surging jets and tumbling droplets, while the still water of the canals mirrored the sky, inducing a more reflective mood. Single jets falling into pools, like the pair in the smaller hanging, were popular in large and small gardens, but even more to be admired were fountains with aqueous figures of tritons, sea horses and river gods pouring forth water from multiple jets. The cupid riding a dolphin in the Orangery Garden fountain provides a focal point in the parterre design, backed up by the pair of statues on tall pedestals.

Statues representing the Roman gods and goddesses were much in vogue, and in the Orangery Garden we see Mercury and Ganymede, the messenger and cup-bearer of Jupiter, presiding over the parterre. At the entrance to the garden a pair of heraldic lions stand guard one on either side of a handsome wrought-iron gate painted a soft grey-blue, similar in tone to the subtle grey used on the magnificent screens made for Hampton Court by the French smith Jean Tijou. They can be seen in the Privy Garden, their scrolling design echoing the box embroidery that adorned the parterres in William and Mary's day, and, like the espaliered fruit, ribbon-like borders and topiary of the Grand Manner, suggesting all sorts of possibilities for contemporary pattern-making.

Fountains playing in patterns drawn by Belinda Downes

CHAPTER 4

Georgian Gardens

'All that luxurious fancy can invent,

What poets feign and painters represent'

<small>ANONYMOUS POEM IN PRAISE OF CASTLE HOWARD ADDRESSED TO LORD CARLISLE, 1733</small>

THE LURE OF CHINOISERIE

In 1694 Sarah Thurstone completed a coverlet in brilliant coloured silks on white satin. In the central garland she placed a tiny figure of a man crossing a bridge towards a cottage with curiously tip-tilted eaves. Apart from an oak tree and some native roses and pinks in the garland, he is alone in a world as alluringly strange as those seen decorating the lustrous surface of lacquer cabinets and and porcelain vases. Around him, the exotic flowers and birds and the gay pavilions with pennants fluttering from their fanciful roofs conjure up the world of far Cathay which had entranced the Western imagination since the days of Marco Polo. This remote land resembled an oriental paradise garden, more sophisticated and elegant than the biblical Garden of Eden and even richer in mysterious decorative motifs. Whether their origin was Chinese, Japanese or Indian, they were found equally intriguing.

A tent stitch panel, one of a pair worked in about 1700, shows how embroiderers combined these motifs to create frivolous garden vignettes which were vaguely but deliciously oriental in mood. Here characters in Eastern dress catch fish, pick fruit and enjoy themselves amid palm trees, exotic birds, fretwork bridges and pavilions perched on rocky outcrops. Early in the eighteenth century these

The design of Sarah Thurstone's coverlet reflects the fascination with the Orient pervading all the decorative arts at the turn of the century. Similar exotic flowers, birds and pavilions ornamented porcelain, tapestries and lacquerware

Garden vignettes with pavilions and lattice bridges, plants and birds decorated lacquer screens, cabinets and porcelain pots like those depicted in this pair of panels, c.1700, in the style of a Soho tapestry. Instead of using realistic perspective (as in the Stoke Edith hangings on pages 73 and 74), oriental designers created appealingly novel visual effects in the asymmetrical but perfectly balanced arrangement of the motifs, disparate elements in a fantasy garden best visited on a flying carpet – perhaps the Chinaman in the centre is unrolling one.

Motifs of a pagoda and multi-flowering tree drawn by Belinda Downes from the exquisite Chinese embroidery on the Calke Abbey bed hangings, c.1700

Motifs from Stalker and Parker's Treatise of Japanning and Varnishing *of 1688*

buildings had no counterpart in real gardens, except perhaps in pheasantries where rare birds were kept, less striking in appearance than the dazzling creatures of needlework. Similar birds swooped and preened themselves on Indian chintzes and Chinese embroideries whose 'splendour and vividness', according to John Evelyn in 1664, 'excell anything seen in Europe'. Embroiderers drew inspiration from these marvellous textiles and from the lacquerwork, wallpaper and porcelain to be seen in fashionable houses. The refulgent surface of lacquerwork made the garden vignettes seem even more mysterious and appealing, and soon an imitation lacquer was developed so that amateurs could do their own 'japanning'. Sensing a craze, John Stalker and George Parker produced their *Treatise on Japanning and Varnishing* in 1688, a treasury of oriental motifs for would-be japanners, but equally suitable for embroiderers in search of pavilions and pagodas.

More authentic views of Chinese buildings and garden features might also have been adapted from the illustrations in *The Embassy to the Grand Tartar* by the Dutchman John Nieuhof, which caused immense excitement when it was translated into English in 1669. There were pagodas galore, and strange 'artificial hills' similar to the rocky outcrops embroidered on Sarah Thurstone's coverlet or the panel on page 81. 'All that see them are surprised with admiration,' wrote Nieuhof, describing the artificial hills as one of the most exciting features of Chinese gardens. In embroidery hilly outcrops appeared in crewel and in whitework, where they were ingeniously patterned and cut into small caverns sheltering diminutive animals and plants. The whitework scenes convey the airy flimsiness of chinoiserie which characterized the real fishermen's houses and the bridges and pavilions that were beginning to appear in eighteenth-century gardens.

It was the irregularity of Chinese gardens that intrigued British garden enthusiasts. The Chinese ideal of beauty was based on asymmetry, and was thus the exact opposite of the regular, symmetrical designs derived from French formal gardens that were advocated by London and Wise and their followers. Chinese designers, as Sir William Temple was the first to point out, scorned the uniformity of 'walks and trees ranged so, as to answer one another,

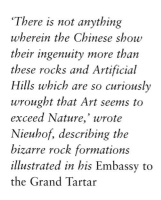

'There is not anything wherein the Chinese show their ingenuity more than these rocks and Artificial Hills which are so curiously wrought that Art seems to exceed Nature,' wrote Nieuhof, describing the bizarre rock formations illustrated in his Embassy to the Grand Tartar

and at exact distances'. They considered this kind of layout child's play in contrast to their own highly sophisticated garden designs which were arranged irregularly 'without order or Disposition of Parts'. This altogether superior kind of beauty was described as *Sharawadgi*, an incomprehensible term for Western gardeners which Temple explained by comparing it to 'the work upon the best *Indian* gowns, or the the painting upon their best Skreens [see the charming example in the left-hand panel on page 81, with its asymmetrical but balanced design] or Purcellans [porcelain]'.

We can see exactly what he meant in the embroidery of an extraordinary dress in the Victoria & Albert Museum on which the decoration resembles that of a chintz or Indian gown. The back is worked with chinoiserie buildings and irregular rockwork sprouting curvaceous stems of exotic flowers and leaves, reminiscent of the crewelwork which was much in fashion at the turn of the century. The style of the dress suggests that it was made up later, some time in the 1750s, and by then chinoiserie buildings, some as strange and ramshackle as those in the embroidery, were appearing everywhere in English gardens. 'There are several paltry Chinese buildings and bridges which have the merit or demerit of being the progenitors of a very numerous race over all the Kingdom,' wrote

Detail of an early eighteenth-century whitework apron delicately embroidered with fishermen perched on rocks 'rarely adorned with Trees and Flowers'

Chinoiserie pavilions and a fretwork fence embroidered

in coloured silks and silver gilt thread adorn this remarkable rococo dress. An avenue of trees 'ranged so… at exact distances' like those in the Stoke Edith hangings ornament the back – a comment perhaps on changing fashions

Horace Walpole in 1753. Three years previously he was less disparaging, saying that these 'dispersed buildings' gave a 'whimsical air of novelty that is very pleasing'. Anyone seeing the pagoda at Kew Gardens (built in 1761) is likely to be struck by its 'whimsical air', even though it has lost the tinkling bells and golden dragons that once decorated the painted roofs. Visitors to Kew in the 1760s would have been able to see a whole variety of 'oriental' buildings including an enchanting pavilion reached by a fretwork bridge. This was in the Pheasant Garden and designed, like the Pagoda, by Sir William Chambers, who was considered an authority on Chinese gardens as he had actually been to China.

As in embroidery, so in gardens; designers used the

decorative features of chinoiserie but arranged them in a frivolous manner remote from the complexity and symbolism of real Chinese gardens like those surrounding the Imperial Palace at Peking. At Stourhead in Wiltshire a wealthy amateur designer, Henry Hoare, created a serpentine lake from the old seventeenth-century fish ponds. Along the walks that encircled it he placed a series of garden buildings ranging in mood from the grandeur of the Pantheon to the simplicity of the rustic cottage and the oriental whimsicality of the steeply arched 'Chinese' bridge, the 'Turkish' tent and the 'Chinese' parasol. The last three soon collapsed, but the rocky grotto, as wonderfully fanciful as Nieuhof's artificial hills or their embroidered counterparts, remains for us to admire, as mysterious as when it was made.

We can see similar features on quilts, coverlets and petticoats and, most enchanting of all, in the paintings of Thomas Robins who recorded vignettes of newly laid out rococo gardens like those at Woodside Old Windsor and Painswick in Gloucestershire in the 1750s. He framed his views in ravishingly pretty borders of trailing periwinkles, jasmine and honeysuckle entwined with stems of auriculas and pinks, twisting and turning as sinuously as their embroidered counterparts on fashionable dress, or the paths and streams in gardens from which the 'Mathematical Exactness and crimping Stiffness' of the Grand Manner had been banished in favour of the 'aimiable Simplicity of Unadorned Nature'.

Centre *Thomas Robins' view of Honington Hall, Warwickshire and the chinoiserie pavilion at Woodside (left), redrawn by Belinda Downes to suggest stitchery*

RURAL LANDSKIPS

'There is a new taste in gardening just arisen,' wrote Sir Thomas Robinson in a letter to Lord Carlisle in 1734. More and more gardens were being laid out 'without level or line', a far more agreeable method, 'as when finished it has the appearance of beautiful nature, and without being told one would imagine that art had no part in the finishing, and is according to what one hears of the Chinese, entirely after their models for works of nature, where they never plant in straight lines or make regular designs'. A comparison of Elizabeth Haines' picture of 1720 with Elizabeth Brain's sampler of 1785 shows at a glance what a revolution had taken place in garden design: formality had fallen from favour, and winding

A ha-ha drawn by Felix Kelly

The winding path, unclipped trees and expansive lawn in Elizabeth Brain's sampler, so different in character from Elizabeth Haines' picture, recall the humorous couplet in Alexander Pope's Epistle to Lord Burlington *in which he expresses his distaste for the rigidity of the formal garden: 'Tired of the scene*

Parterres and Fountains yield,/ He finds at last he better likes a Field.' The brighter green strip of grass with deer beyond it suggests the presence of a ha-ha, enabling the owner to merge garden, fields and countryside, and make 'a pretty Landskip of his own Possessions'. To explore the 'landskip', the visitor

followed the path enjoying a variety of viewpoints along the way, in complete contrast to Elizabeth Haines' garden which showed to the best advantage from the viewpoint marked by her initials. Coloured silks on woollen canvas worked in long and short, stem, tent and chain stitches

walks, groves and expansive lawns replaced straight walks, 'clipt plants' and parterres.

The demise of the Grand Manner was hastened by influential writers like Joseph Addison, editor of *The Spectator* (1711–14). In a famous essay published on 25 June 1712 he expressed the growing disenchantment with formal gardens like those in the Stoke Edith hangings, lamenting that 'Our British Gardeners instead of humouring Nature, love to deviate from it as much as possible. Our trees rise in Cones, Globes and Pyramids. We see the Marks of Scissars upon every Plant and Bush. I do not know whether I am singular in my Opinion, but for my part, I would rather look upon a Tree in all its Luxuriancy and Diffusion of Boughs and Branches, than when it is cut and trimmed into a Mathematical Figure; and cannot but fancy that an Orchard in Flower looks infinitely more delightful, than the little labyrinths of the most finished

Parterre'. Addison's seductive descriptions of idealized natural landscapes encouraged a new kind of gardening, persuading his readers to adopt his advice in their properties. 'Why may not a whole Estate be thrown into a Garden...?' he enquired in the same essay. 'Fields of Corn make a pleasant Prospect, and if the Walks were a little taken care of that lie between them, if the natural Embroidery of the Meadows were helpt and improved by some small Additions of Art, and the several Rows of Hedges set off by Trees and Flowers...a Man might make a pretty Landskip of his own Possessions.'

Two years later in October 1714, during a light-hearted correspondence on the 'laudable mystery of embroidery', Addison was advocating similar 'Landskips' as a 'delightful entertainment' for needlewomen: 'Your pastoral poetesses may vent their fancy in rural landscapes, and place despairing shepherds under silken willows, or drown them in a sea of mohair,' he teased, commenting on the numerous Arcadian scenes he saw in embroidery: 'How pleasing is the amusement of walking among the shades and groves planted by themselves, in surveying heroes slain by their needle, or little cupids which they have brought into the world without pain.'

The real rural landscape changed dramatically during the early years of the eighteenth century as a result of government policy to enclose the common land and improve turf for grazing. Gradually a patchwork of well-kept fields divided by hedges spread over land that had formerly been bog and 'all horrid and woody', and thickets were planted for the benefit of huntsmen who now chased after devious foxes instead of galloping headlong down straight drives after stags. The countryside was no longer hostile; it was as well ordered as the land within the garden walls, but it avoided all 'abominable Mathematical Regularity and Stiffness'. The novel idea of merging the garden and the countryside, 'calling in the country', in Alexander Pope's expressive phrase, appealed not only to the imagination but to the pocket also. Many garden owners, weary of the 'Lothsome Burden' of expense in maintaining their parterres of embroidery, miles of clipped hedges, topiary and exotics, were probably swayed as much by thoughts of economy as by boredom with the old style when they set about digging up the parterres, pulling down walls and felling the avenues.

The argument of economy was temptingly proposed by Stephen Switzer in 1715 in *The Nobleman, Gentleman and Gardener's Recreation*. He recommended that 'all the adjacent country should be laid open to the view of the eye, and should not be bounded by high walls', and he named the device that made this possible and practical, the ha-ha, ' an easy unaffected manner of Fencing to make the adjacent country look as if it were all a garden'. He failed to mention that the fence needed to be sunk below eye level in a ditch which kept deer, cattle and sheep away from the vicinity of the house but gave the inhabitants the illusion that the land beyond was part of the garden.

There is no way of knowing whether there are ha-has in the rural 'Landskips' of Georgian needlework, for they could be easily concealed behind the rows of hillocks that at first sight appear identical to those of the previous century. Nor has the embroiderer entirely abandoned the cast of biblical and mythological personages, but they have been overtaken by others, skittishly dressed as shepherds and shepherdesses, most suitable characters for the 'farm-like way of Gardening' recommended by Switzer. They can be seen in innumerable embroidered pictures, on panels for sconces and screens, inside card tables and on sofas and chairs. Tent stitch was back in fashion, and once again the scenes worked on furnishings throughout the house echoed a child's-eye view of the latest gardens which were being laid out to give the illusion of an Arcadian landscape as idealized as the paintings of Claude Lorrain.

'Landscape should contain variety enough to form a picture upon canvas; and this is no bad test, as I think the landskip painter is the gardener's best designer,' wrote

Opposite 'Rural Landskip' in an early eighteenth-century tent stitch picture evocative of scenes in the newly fashionable ornamental farm

Chair cover worked by the 11-year-old Eleanor Bowes, recording the garden features in the landscape garden at Gibside in Northumberland laid out in 1761

William Shenstone in *Unconnected Thoughts on Gardening*, published in 1764. He had put his theory into practice in his own garden, the Leasowes near Birmingham, developed imaginatively but at modest cost in the 1740s. Wealthier garden owners tried even harder than Shenstone to re-create the Claudian landscapes which hung in their country houses as evocative memories of the Italian scenery with its classical ruins which they had admired on the Grand Tour. Shenstone had never been to Italy and he contented himself by evoking the spirit of the idyllic painted land-scapes, ingeniously reorganizing his 60-hectare (150-acre) estate so that the visitor followed a path leading from one viewpoint to another, enjoying a series of apparently natural but in fact most carefully contrived scenes. Each scene prompted different responses and reflections, appealing as much to the mind and emotions as to the eye. Shenstone called his garden a *ferme ornée*, or ornamental farm, as it encompassed fields of grazing sheep and cattle – idyllic, tranquil vignettes in contrast to 'wilder scenes' made solemn with urns, ruins and appropriate inscriptions.

The charm of the Leasowes, and of the first *ferme ornée*, Woburn Farm in Surrey, laid out by Philip Southcote from the mid-1730s, is preserved in the rural scenes of needle-work. Southcote's original desire for making improvements was 'joined to a taste for the more simple delights of the

Idealized views of the 'farm-like way of gardening' were favourite subjects for Georgian embroiderers. This early eighteenth-century picture brings alive Thomas Whately's description of Woburn Farm: 'With the beauties which enliven a garden are everwhere intermixed many properties which enliven a farm; both the lawns are fed [grazed], and the lowing of the herds, and bleeting of the sheep … resound all round the plantations.' The ruins inspired more sombre thoughts

country … as a means of bringing every rural circumstance within the verge of the garden'. Thomas Whately has left us a picture of Woburn in his *Observations on Modern Gardening* of 1770. He admired the changing prospect of cornfields, grazing cattle, poultry in a menagerie near a Gothic building, waterfowl on a 'small serpentine river', and remarked how 'a peculiar cheerfulness overspreads the lawns arising from the number and splendour of the objects with which they abound'.

It is this cheerfulness that the embroidered *fermes ornées* capture. They evoke carefree summer days when time steals away, and it is pleasant to rest on the grass listening to the sound of the sheep, and water flowing along a 'little wandering rill … through banks of violets and primroses'.

Above Visitors *followed a circular path starting from the house to enjoy the delights of Woburn Farm: 'the scenes through which it leads are truly elegant, everywhere rich and always agreeable. On the way round the garden they were presented with a variety of visual surprises including temples and scenes reminiscent of Italian paintings*

Shepherds and shepherdesses sit by their flocks dressed in clothes as pretty and frivolous as those in the paintings of Watteau or Boucher, which, as Horace Walpole remarked, 'betray more wealthy expense than is consistent with the economy of a Farmer, or the rusticity of labour'. He was describing Woburn, 'Mr Southcote's ornamental farm where he displayed his peculiar style with happiness and taste...

Pastoral scenes delighted poets and artists, as in this detail of William Kent's illustration of 'Spring' from Thomson's Seasons, *1742*

'The natural embroidery of
the meadows' makes a
charming background for a
shepherdess in this mid-
eighteenth-century tent stitch
picture

[it was] the habitation of such nymphs and shepherds as are represented in landscapes and novels, but do not exist in real life'. Yet silken shepherds and shepherdesses *were* sometimes seen in real gardens in his day, taking part in *fêtes champêtres* as enthusiastically as their ancestors had done in the masques and revels of previous centuries.

Mrs Delany, diarist, embroiderer, maker of gardens, shell grottoes and cut paper flowers and an inveterate party-goer, described a ball at Delville, her home near Dublin in 1752 'with musicians and singers dressed like Arcadian shepherds and shepherdesses placed among the rocks'. In July 1774 she enjoyed another 'fairy scene' at Lady Betty Hamilton's *fête champêtre*: 'The company was received on the lawn before the house, which is scattered with trees and opens to the downs. The company arriving, and partys of people of all ranks that came to admire made the scene quite enchanting.' An impromptu stage in another part of the garden, concealed 'with sticks entwined with natural flowers in wreaths and festoons', was the setting for a 'little dialogue between a Shepherd and Shepherdess', and then musicians and dancers from the Opera entertained the guests who were 'very elegantly dressed: the very young as peasants … and *many gardeners, as in the opera dances*'.

Dear Mrs Delany

But here the needle plies its busy task,
The pattern grows, the well-depict'd flower
Unfolds its bosom, buds and leaves and sprigs,
And curling tendrils, gracefully disposed,
Follow the nimble fingers of the fair;
A wreath that cannot fade, of flowers that blow
With most success when all besides decay.

William Cowper finished this poem, 'The Task', in 1784 when Mrs Delany was 84 years old. Throughout her long life her needle 'plied its busy task' in embroidery that was extraordinarily varied and individual. Never happier than when she was busy, she worked in white on the finest lawn and muslin, and with coloured silks and worsteds (specially made for her in Ireland) on canvas and on silk and woollen grounds. She also enjoyed knotting and spinning and helped her husband, Doctor Patrick Delany, in making their garden at Delville at Glasnevin in Ireland. She was an ardent flower enthusiast and like John Gerard, whose herbal she admired, she valued the links between embroidery and gardens. The flowers she worked herself and her remarks on other people's embroidered dress and

Detail of an Irish linen coverlet worked in knotting by Mrs Delany as a present for Thomas Sandford in 1765

Right *A hyacinth on Mrs Delany's court dress, its broken leaf meticulously recorded in long and short stitches*

furnishings make interesting comment on the plants then in fashion and how they were displayed.

Her great-grandniece, Lady Llanover, wrote a description of the flowers she embroidered on the petticoat of her court dress which might serve as a plant list and guide for re-creating a small flower garden of the kind enthusiasts continued to cultivate and enjoy in defiance of the 'landskip' fashion. The petticoat was covered with sprays of natural flowers including bugloss, auriculas, honeysuckle, wild roses, lilies of the valley and yellow and white jasmine, interspersed with small single flowers. The border at the bottom was entirely composed of 'large flowers in the manner in which they grow, both *garden* and *wild* flowers being intermingled where the form, proportions and foliage rendered it desirable for the effect of the whole'. The petticoat with its border of auriculas, primulas, horned poppy and geranium has survived, the delightfully informal arrangement of the flowers concealing the

Detail of a horned poppy and polyanthus in the flower border on the petticoat of Mrs Delany's court dress.

The embroidery conveys the luxuriant effect she loved in her borders and shrubberies at Delville

carefully planned design. We may imagine that the shrubberies at Delville were thought out with equal care.

At a party in 1740, Mrs Delany was particularly struck by the fanciful treatment of weeds and wild flowers on the Duchess of Queensbury's highly individual clothes, so much so that she wished she had thought of it first. These 'were white satin embroidered, the bottom of the petticoat *brown hills* covered with all sorts of weeds and *every breadth* had *an old stump of a tree* that ran almost to the top of the petticoat, broken and wragged and worked with brown chenille, round which twined nasturtians, ivy, honeysuckles, periwinkles, convolvuluses, and all sorts of twining flowers which spread and covered the petticoat...'

Perhaps the design appealed to her as a witty topical reference to the dead trees set out by the landscape gardener William Kent in Kensington Gardens, where they were intended to imitate nature and 'give a greater truth to the scene'. Kent's ruling principle was that 'Nature abhors a straight line', and in gardens and in needlework this led to much pretty meandering. Like the sinuous rivers, streams and paths in the landscape garden, the stems, foliage and flowers on dresses, carpets and cushions twisted and turned as naturally as if they had been tossed from a shepherdess's basket onto the ground.

We can see the picturesque effect in Mrs Delany's drawings of her own garden at Delville. It was 4.5 hectares (11 acres) in size, resembling a modest ornamental farm, with grazing deer, meandering streams and an island with swans. The Delanys often took their meals out of doors, where a musical accompaniment was provided by an Irish harpist. They grew quantities of different flowers and fruits, and in 1750 Mrs Delany was 'considering about a greenhouse'. She wrote, 'I believe I shall build one this spring; my orange trees thrive *so well* they deserve one'. They made a 'nine pin bowling alley for very merry exercise' and entertained their numerous friends. Sadly their taste for trying out novelties and making improvements ended in financial disaster, and when he died in 1768, a wag wrote that Doctor Delany was 'Quite ruin'd and bankrupt reduced to a farthing/ By making too much of a very small garden'.

Mrs Delany returned to England after his death, and contented herself with other people's gardens, especially those of her closest friend the Duchess of Portland, at Bulstrode near Gerrards Cross. The Duchess shared many of her interests, and they botanized, sketched and enjoyed each other's conversation while Mrs Delany sat at her spinning wheel or embroidery, or made candelabras of shellwork for her friend's house.

Her feeling for plants and nature, her talent for design and her interest in changing attitudes to the landscape garden all influenced Mrs Delany's embroidery, and she would have agreed wholeheartedly with the anonymous poet celebrating Castle Howard when he wrote 'O'er all Designs Nature should still preside/ She is the cheapest and most perfect Guide'. She was, however, well aware of the pitfalls of following the Guide too closely. Lady Llanover constantly drew attention to the naturalness of Mrs Delany's work, but her descriptions and Mrs Delany's own comments suggest that her gift lay in absorbing every detail of what she saw and then formalizing it to suit a particular piece of work, choosing exactly appropriate stitches, colours and materials. Her originality and skill can still be admired in the flowers she cut from paper, an activity she did not begin until her seventies. As in her embroidery, each flower is a true but at the same time decorative portrait of the plant – a most difficult ideal to achieve, as anyone who has tried it will know. Her enthusiastic delight in something new is typical, as is the perfection of her technique and her perseverance in carrying out her projects. Yet even she sometimes found the completion of a piece of embroidery tedious. 'It is provoking,' she wrote, 'to have the ground take up so much more time than the flowers' – a thought that often crosses my mind at the start of a weeding session.

The 'Swift and Swans' Island' at Delville, drawn by Mrs Delany in 1745. 'The rurality of it is wonderfully pretty,' she wrote, describing how the garden preserved the wildness of nature, 'so that you would not imagine it to be a work of art.' Visitors could follow 'little wild walks' along the winding brook which ran through the garden

PLEASING MELANCHOLY

Mrs Delany was a keen garden visitor, noting the 'improvements' she saw with interest. In the spring of 1733 she remarked on the straight canals, temples and formally arranged statues at Dangan, not far from Delville, but when she returned in the autumn of 1748 further improvements had taken place. The canals had been replaced by a natural-looking lake, and there were woodland walks with seats strategically placed for visitors to rest and enjoy the changing prospects; the statues now marked the best viewpoints, together with obelisks and pillars.

Like the urns, ruins, hermitages and grottoes that were now, in Mrs Malaprop's words, 'the very pineapple of fashion', these features were skilfully sited in different parts of the new landscape gardens to indicate different moods and associations. There were ruins and urns at both the Leasowes and Woburn Farm, designed to turn the visitors' thoughts from frivolity to melancholy. Passing by open cornfields and happy rural scenes they would suddenly come on a sylvan temple or a solitary urn, complete with an inscription recalling the death of some dearly loved friend. The embroidery on a settee and chair at Marble Hill House reflects the vogue, with vignettes of ruins set among peacefully grazing sheep and goats. The

'Views of Ruins after the old Roman manner for the Termination of Walks, Prospects etc' from New Principles of Gardening *(1728). Batty Langley's suggestion of painting them on canvas as distant eye-* catchers would have appealed to enthusiasts of modest means, though wealthy garden owners did 'actually build' mock ruins. They appear in canvaswork from the 1720s

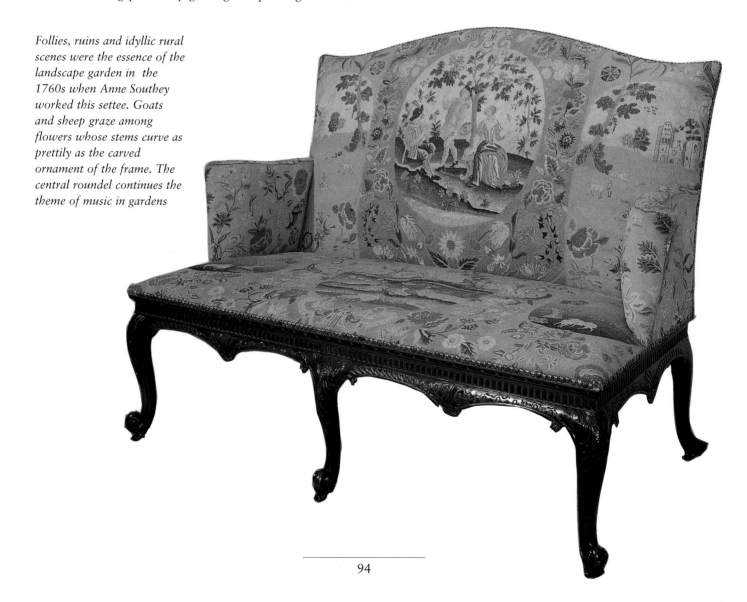

Follies, ruins and idyllic rural scenes were the essence of the landscape garden in the 1760s when Anne Southey worked this settee. Goats and sheep graze among flowers whose stems curve as prettily as the carved ornament of the frame. The central roundel continues the theme of music in gardens

Two hearts burn on an altar dedicated to love in this late eighteenth-century silk picture; drooping willows add melancholy to the scene. Temples dedicated to Venus were built at Stowe and West Wycombe

'Little altar almost in ruins' illustrated in Le Rouge's Jardins Anglo Chinois *inspires sombre thoughts on the passing of time*

inspiration may have come from a real garden, but an equally likely source would be the illustrations of 'Old ruins' in Batty Langley's *New Principles of Gardening*, 'which *Ruins* may be *painted upon Canvas* or actually built'.

'A ruin,' wrote Shenstone, 'may be neither new to us, nor majestic, nor beautiful, yet afford the pleasing melancholy which proceeds from a reflection on decayed magnificence. For this reason an able gardener should avail himself of objects that convey reflections of the pleasing kind.' Georgian embroiderers found the landscape gardener's favourite 'objects' equally pleasing, and used them to create miniature prospects of silken temples overhung with chenille willows, or urns set in glades visited by mournful maidens bringing flowers and garlands. Late eighteenth-century scenes of 'pleasing melancholy' looked charming worked on delicate silk backgrounds using simple straight stitches in silks and chenille. Unlike the earlier rural

Late eighteenth-century silk picture of girls garlanding a monument to departed friends or lovers by a lake in a landscape garden. The scene recalls the winding outlines of the lakes with bridges and waterside paths at Stourhead, West Wycombe and Painshill

landscapes on canvaswork furnishings, the fragile materials made them suitable only to be framed as pictures or the panels for small screens. As in the past, the patterns were often adapted from engravings and book illustrations, and 'picturesque gardening' had become so popular that there was a wealth of motifs to choose from. Some designs were available ready drawn on the silk from specialist shops, but if these did not appeal, the embroiderer could find what she wanted in one of the many new books of designs for garden buildings and ornaments, or in novels or volumes of poetry. She found 'melancholy' of a pleasing or thrilling kind as she lingered over the stanzas of Thompson's *Seasons* (1730) or Gray's *Elegy* (1750), or revelled in the *Mysteries of Udolpho* (1794) by Mrs Radcliffe.

It was tempting to illustrate the romantic scenes in needlework, and most fortunate that this could be done quickly and without a great deal of skill when there were other delightful pastimes such as sketching to dabble in. Generally embroiderers preferred small-scale vignettes of the landscape garden, and made few, if any, attempts to convey either the vastness of the famous gardens laid out by Capability Brown or the paintings of the great landscape artists – Claude Lorrain, Gaspard Poussin and Salvator Rosa – which garden designers had imitated in three-dimensional form in the English countryside. The only notable exception was Miss Morritt of Rokeby, who endeavoured to reproduce the landscapes of Gaspard Poussin in long and short stitch in worsteds in her needle-paintings.

Opposite above Late eighteenth-century sampler recording a whole compendium of 'objects' used by landscape gardeners to convey 'pleasing melancholy', including urns, broken pillars and a small grotto or hermitage overhung with willows

William Woollett's view of the Temple of Venus and bridge at West Wycombe

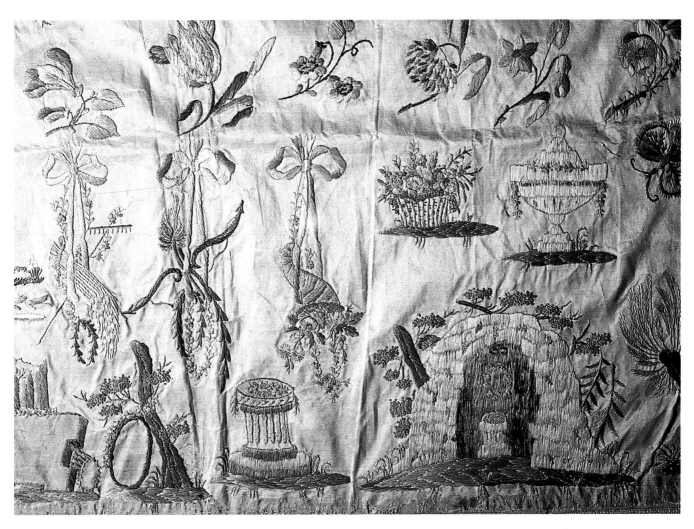

In 1760 Mrs Delany visited Longleat, where the formal garden had been removed in favour of a 'fine lawn, a serpentine river, wooded hills, gravel paths meandering round a shrubbery, all modernised by the ingenious and much sought after Mr Brown'. Not everyone was as enthusiastic and, as in the days of topiary and rigid formality, satirists now found there were just as many absurdities in the landscape garden. Their witty comments sometimes correspond with contemporary pictorial embroidery, with its naïve and frivolous air even in supposedly serious scenes.

'The Hermitage Stanford 1738', drawn by the antiquary William Stukeley, shows ruins and a small structure similar to the grotto embroidered on the sampler shown above. Mrs Delany planned a 'very pretty grotto' in a cave at Delville and real hermits were employed at Richmond and Painshill

Left An obelisk, column, urns and statue drawn by Felix Kelly

Above and opposite *In these chair backs depicting 'The Gardener and the Hog' and 'The Poet and the Rose' from Gay's* Fables *the garden backgrounds record early developments in the landscape style reminiscent of the gardens of Chiswick House in whose design William Kent was extensively involved. Wootton's engraving* (right) *has been reversed in copying by the pattern-drawer*

The garden created by the newly rich Mr Sterling in Garrick and Colman's play *The Clandestine Marriage* of 1766 has echoes in needlework in the choice and over-crowding of decorative elements. Besides a 'little Gothic dairy, an octagonal summer house, a Chinese Bridge, a cascade and ruins which had cost one hundred pounds and fifty pounds to put into repair', there was also a mock spire among the distant trees, masquerading as the parish church. 'One must always have a church, or an obelisk, or something to terminate the prospect, you know...'

A tottering obelisk terminates the prospect on a chair cover adapted from an illustration by John Wootton for 'The Gardener and the Hog' in John Gay's *Fables* (1731). The chair was part of a large set, and the pattern-drawer devised a further design using another illustration, this time by William Kent for the fable of 'The Poet and the Rose'. Kent shows the poet versifying as he plucks a rose, and registers his surprise when another rose in the bed

breaks angrily into speech, reminding him that her blooms are indispensable to poets and that they should not be idly picked and left to die. Both Kent's illustration and the embroidery convey the teasing irony of the fable, and the contrived and crowded garden setting, with its statue, fountain and apparently half-dead tree (another reference to Kent's planting in Kensington Gardens, perhaps) would be equally apt to illustrate the glade in the garden of Squire Mushroom, a would-be amateur of taste mocked in the popular periodical *The World* in 1753. 'After traipsing along the yellow serpentine river' past a hermitage built of roots, his guests, 'almost in despair of ever visiting daylight any more', emerged 'on a sudden into an open and circular area richly chequered with beds of flowers and embellished with a little fountain playing in the centre of it'.

While many garden owners were persuaded to 'improve' their grounds to suit the prevailing taste, others took little notice, and went on cultivating fruit and flowers as they had always done, their only concession to the current trends being to modify their flowerbeds and shrubberies along informal lines. The flood of introductions from all over the world and new varieties of old favourites developed by florists and nurserymen thrilled the plant enthusiasts, and some of their novelties were taken up by embroiderers – Mrs Delany, for example, recording the latest anemones and a pelargonium from South Africa on her petticoat. Flower gardening, according to the Reverend John Bennett (in *Letters to a Young Lady*, 1795) was 'a truly feminine amusement. If you mix it with taste for botany and a knowledge of plants you will never be in want of an excellent restorative'. The restorative quality of both gardening and needlework was to be enjoyed by many more enthusiasts – both men and women – in the coming century.

Italian woodcut, c.1770

CHAPTER 5

Regency and Victorian Gardens

'The garden is an artificial contrivance…a creation of art, not of wild nature'
SHIRLEY HIBBERD, *RUSTIC ADORNMENT FOR HOMES OF TASTE,* 1856

CARPET BEDDING AND BERLIN WOOLWORK

In the last years of the eighteenth century many gardens had become so 'natural' that critics claimed they were indistinguishable from the surrounding countryside. The vast landscapes of Capability Brown put Mr Milestone, the hero of Thomas Peacock's satire *Headlong Hall* (1816), in mind of 'big bowling greens, like sheets of green paper, with a parcel of round clumps scattered over them like so many spots of ink, flicked at random out of a pen, and a solitary animal here and there looking as if it was lost'. The effect was 'for all the world like Hounslow Heath, thinly sprinkled over with bushes and highwaymen'. Mr Milestone is a landscape gardener, intended by Peacock as a caricature of Humphry Repton (1782–1818), Brown's most famous follower, and the man responsible for gradually turning the tide of taste away from 'bald and bare landscapes' towards 'interesting pleasure grounds' closely related to the house, and designed to combine convenience and utility with beauty. Repton reintroduced flowerbeds near the house and kept Brown's lawns at bay with terraces; formal trelliswork festooned with roses, jasmine and honeysuckle matched the symmetry of the neo-classical architecture; and even the long-banished fountain, symbol of artifice and unnatural constraint, was allowed to return.

Repton's suggestions for reintroducing formal elements near the house were seized on with enthusiasm by owners of large estates and smaller properties alike. His ideas were

Berlin-work picture of a fountain framed in a border of flowers in plushwork

A fountain illustrated in The Ladies' Companion *of 1850, edited by Mrs Loudon*

A trellis 'window' garlanded with
roses heightens the picturesque effect
of the ribbon borders and statues
in the garden at Trentham Hall
illustrated in E. Adveno Brooke's The
Gardens of England, 1857

particularly welcome to the growing, affluent and educated middle classes, the owners of Regency and early Victorian villas, whose properties were not large enough to embrace the spacious wildness of the landscape garden, and whose wives now preferred a 'dressed' flower garden and 'gravel rather than grass paths covered in dew'. The pleasing effect, with nature 'corrected – trimmed – polished – decorated and adorned' to borrow Mr Milestone's phrase, can be seen in Mary Pether's sampler of 1839, where the people are in no danger of getting their feet wet, and the makers of countless other early nineteenth-century samplers which likewise show house and garden prettily reunited, set off with 'rich embellishments' in the shape of ornamental shrubberies and pots and baskets of flowers.

Anne Curren's sampler of 1837 depicts 'smooth gravel walks' winding in 'a graceful, easy manner' between shrubberies of mixed trees, bushes and flowers as advocated by John Claudius Loudon (1783–1843), soon to take over from Repton as the foremost garden expert of the time. Her embroidery accurately records the picturesque type of shrubbery coming into vogue in parks and gardens. Here evergreen shrubs are combined with small trees and

herbaceous plants, evoking the irregular thickets of a forest lawn or woodland glade, but planted with a far wider variety of 'shrubs of the most elegant sort', including exotic newcomers from abroad.

Practical advice on planting shrubberies and all aspects of horticulture was to be found in the flood of magazines and handbooks written to instruct and encourage the growing numbers of 'suburban gardeners', as Loudon called the new villa owners.

Some publications were intended specifically for ladies, and it is intriguing to see how often the practicalities of gardening were clarified through reference to needlework. In 1841 a reader wrote to the *Ladies' Magazine of Gardening*, edited by Loudon's wife Jane, with this query: 'I am desirous of gaining a little information as to the planting of a geometrical flower garden with the *gayest* and *brightest* colours.'

Mrs Loudon explained 'how the ground must be levelled, and the plan, if complicated traced upon it. Having divided the plan into an equal number of squares by lines drawn on the paper, copy what is found on a large scale in every square. This is difficult to describe, but it

Opposite *Mary Pether's sampler records a typical villa garden laid out for the convenience and pleasure of its owners with gravel paths, 'a sweet little lawn', ornamental arches, seats and flower baskets. Humphry Repton introduced the idea of small round beds planted to resemble living flower baskets on the lawn near the house; one can be seen in Mrs Loudon's* Gardening for Ladies *on page 105*

Anne Curren's sampler (right) *depicts a domed building, possibly based on a print of George III's Observatory in the Old Deer Park at Kew. The shrubbery walks might have been stitched following Henry Phillips' advice for 'gardeners of villas and ornamental cottages' in* Sylva Florifera *published in 1823: 'The picture should be formed by judiciously contrasting the greens.' As he recommended, Mary Curren uses varying shades to create a lively, perspectival effect*

Houses with neat gardens were a feature in Regency samplers, many of which were embellished with baskets of flowers. Belinda Downes shows how these motifs might be developed as a border design

Ann Curren Her Work Finished March The 7. 1837 Aged 13 Years

will be easy in practice to anyone who has been accustomed to copying worsted work patterns drawn on Berlin paper'.

The great majority of Mrs Loudon's readers would have grasped what she meant at once, as copying brightly coloured Berlin patterns in tent or cross stitch was rapidly becoming a craze. These were first imported from Berlin in 1804, and by the 1840s there was a huge choice

available in specialist shops like Wilks' Warehouse in Regent Street in London, together with a seductive range of wools, canvas and other accessories. 'This fashionable tapestry work,' noted Mrs Stone, the editor of *The Art of Needlework* (the first history of embroidery, published in 1840), 'seems quite to have usurped the place of the various other embroideries that have from time to time occupied the leisure moments of the fair.' Though the glaring brightness of the colours was not to Mrs Stone's taste, and though she agreed that the stitching might be considered mechanical, she still found 'infinitely more scope for fancy, taste and even genius' in Berlin woolwork than in the silk pictures (see pages 95 and 96) whose popularity had been eclipsed by the new craze. Few would share her opinion today, for the silk pictures left some room for personal choice in colours and stitches, whereas copying a Berlin pattern was about as individual as painting by numbers.

The same might be said about the 'geometrical' flower garden designs in which not only the layout but the choice of flowers and colours too could be copied direct from a plan in a book or magazine. Whether such a plan was transferred to the garden or to canvas, the method was identical. Mrs Loudon's instructions were designed to help ladies whose expertise in Berlin woolwork might exceed their knowledge of practical gardening. She knew nothing at all about the latter subject when she married John Loudon, though she was already a successful writer, having first met her husband at a reading of her eerie novel *The Mummy*. Loudon was eager to instruct her, and soon she was not only helping to tend the vast range of plants in the garden of their house in Bayswater, but taking down the text of his books late into the night. In her first book on horticulture, *Gardening for Ladies*, she branched out on her own, determined to share the knowledge she had

Right 'Basketwork' beds in Mrs Lawrence's garden at Drayton Green. The Loudons visited in 1833, finding it 'a perfect bijou of floricultural beauty'. The intricate triangular beds (below) reminded them of the lace collars in van Dyck's portraits

Opposite *The brilliant colours of the Berlin patterns – as shown in this flower-basket design – contributed to the immense popularity of this type of woolwork*

Above *The title page of Mrs Loudon's* Gardening for Ladies *(1840) depicts a lady contemplating a flower-basket bed, 'constructed with curved pieces of iron' stuck into the ground', which,* *when planted, would resemble a real basket set down on the lawn; a wire handle entwined with climbers completed the picturesque effect. Mrs Loudon also recommended wicker hanging baskets for greenhouses. Baskets in variety appear in countless nineteenth-century samplers, echoing the popularity of those in gardens*

Motif from the title page of
The Ladies' Companion,
edited by Mrs Loudon

Right *Groups of spring flowers and initial letters from the 'Work Basket' column in* The Ladies' Companion. *Worked in satin stitch on muslin, they would*

be *'exceedingly suitable for pocket handkerchiefs to be worn at the floral fêtes at the Horticultural and Botanical Gardens'*

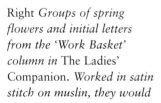

Far left *Geometric Berlin design from* The Young Ladies' Journal. *Each square represented a cross or tent stitch, and by careful counting it was quick and easy to copy the design onto canvas*

Left *Geometrical flower gardens similar in effect to the Berlin pattern shown left, illustrated in an article by Jane Loudon in* The Ladies' Companion. *She listed the flowers that were to be used, indicating their place on the plan so that it was as easy to follow as a Berlin design*

The embroidery-like effect of massed bedding is well illustrated in the Alhambra Garden at Elvaston Castle in E. Adveno Brooke's The Gardens of England

acquired during 10 years of hard work and show her female readers how they too might exercise their 'skill and ingenuity' in this pleasurable pursuit.

The book was exactly what the Victorian lady with an interest in flowers and plenty of time to spend in her garden needed. With the advent of the Industrial Revolution, garden-making, like embroidery, was no longer the exclusive preserve of the nobility and gentry. 'Opulent commercial men,' as Loudon referred to the newly rich middle classes, bought his book *The Suburban Gardener and Villa Gardener*, published in 1836, for advice on embellishing their grounds, while their wives preferred Mrs Loudon's publications as they were less formidable and her enthusiasm and clear instructions inspired confidence. In *The Villa Companion* (1850) she again chose the comparison of embroidery to encourage her readers to lay out their own flower gardens: 'The skill required to do so is within the capacity of every woman who can work or embroider patterns for the different parts of a female dress; and supposing a female to have grown up without the slightest knowledge of the art of working a pattern, or tracing out a flower garden, it would certainly be much easier for her to acquire the latter art than the former... We venture to assert that there is not any lady who can design a pattern and embroider a gown, that might not, in a few hours, be taught to design flower gardens with as much taste and skill as a professional landscape gardener.'

In 1850 Mrs Loudon edited *The Ladies' Companion*, a magazine with stories, poems and reviews as well as articles on embroidery and gardening. In some issues the 'Work Basket' section lies adjacent to her articles on aspects of 'The Garden' as if to suggest that they were connected. In an article on the flower garden, Mrs Loudon explained the difference between a mixed and a geometrical flower garden, with plans and plant lists for the latter. 'In a geometrical flower garden,' she wrote, 'the colours must be contrived to produce a striking effect contrasted with each other, and the plants must be chosen as to be nearly of the same size, so that the garden when seen at a distance may have the effect of a Turkey carpet' – or of Berlin woolwork, whose patterns and colours were strikingly similar to those of the carpet bedding in the geometrical garden.

Geometrical gardens with massed bedding became fashionable in the 1830s, when Berlin woolwork was becoming all the rage. The plants were laid out in patterns reminiscent of the earlier knots or parterres but the effect was quite different because of the brilliant colours of the new bedding plants, many of them tender and half-hardy varieties forced and brought on in the greenhouses which were one of the wonders of the age. In the late 1860s a new type of bedding using dwarf foliage plants such as *Echeveria* and *Alternanthera* made its appearance, aptly

named 'carpet' or 'tapestry' bedding, because the neat low-growing plants could delineate complex patterns similar to Turkey carpets and Berlin woolwork. Another variant was 'leaf embroidery' bedding, described by Shirley Hibberd in the *The Amateur's Flower Garden*, published in 1871. Here only foliage plants with their flowers picked off were used, and it was 'equally well adapted to the greatest terrace garden or the quite humble and unpretending grass plot in a villa garden. It may be likened in a general way to a hearthrug or Turkey carpet pattern'. Hibberd referred his readers to an article in the *Floral World* of 1871 where this type of bedding was described in full. It bore 'such general resemblance to embroidery as to justify the name by which this system is to be henceforth known'. The displays of embroidery in the subtropical garden at Battersea Park were particularly 'rich and tasteful'.

Leaf embroidery was designed to produce 'sheets of colour', and its novelty lay in being slightly more muted than the 'dazzling' effects of the previous decades. In *The Amateur's Flower Garden* Hibberd also described a 'curious and eminently pleasing style of massing known as tessellated colouring, the colours being repeated in small blotches with sharp dividing lines to separate the groups'. It sounds remarkably similar in effect to the geometrical patterns in popular women's periodicals such as *The Englishwoman's Domestic Magazine* and *The Young Ladies' Journal*. A number of these also resemble the re-introduced parterre designs, using box embroidery and coloured sands in the French formal style. These had, as Shirley Hibberd said, the 'advantage that, during winter, it affords "something to look at", but the corresponding disadvantage is that nobody wants to see it'.

The connections between geometrical gardens with massed bedding and Berlin woolwork remained remarkably close throughout the 50 years when both were in favour,

Left 'The Campana Circular Design' echoes the effect of 'The White Sand Garden' (right) illustrated in David Thomson's The Handy Book of the Flower Garden. *The garden pattern was marked out on the ground from the squared-up plan exactly as one might copy 'the paper containing plans for Berlin worsted work' as Mrs Loudon explained in* The Ladies' Companion to the Flower Garden

and changes of fashion in flowers, colours and patterns appeared in each of them almost simultaneously as if by some curious cross-fertilization. The brightest possible colours were admired during the 1860s and into the 1870s, when more muted shades were introduced, and the most complicated geometrical patterns for Berlin woolwork also coincided with the most intricate effects in the garden. There were corresponding echoes too in the choice of flowers. In the 1830s the embroidered flowers tended to be old favourites like roses, pansies, auriculas and poppies, which were equally popular in the garden. With the development of greenhouse culture, gaily coloured annuals and showy exotics joined these favourites which had themselves become blowsy and inflated-looking, as if in competition with the newcomers. Arum lilies and fuchsias in vibrant reds and purple were prized as much by needlewomen as by gardeners, and appeared in patterns and illustrations in magazines and books on both subjects.

In *The Ladies' Country Companion* published in 1845, Mrs Loudon gave advice to Annie, a newly married friend who had given up town life for a home in the country and was thoroughly miserable as a result. Mrs Loudon encouraged Annie to transform her husband's gloomy and neglected garden, and showed her how to lay out a geometrical flower garden. So well did she succeed that soon it was 'so brilliant with bright scarlet verbenas and golden yellow calceolarias that you can scarcely gaze at it in the sunshine'. Flowers as overpoweringly bright as those

Brilliantly coloured flowers worked in plush stitch created inflated, domed effects reminiscent of carpet bedding. Plush stitch was worked by looping the wool round a gage and then cutting and fluffing it up

she described were further intensified in needlework by the contrast of a dark ground. This set them off as handsomely as the velvety lawns – now cut smooth by the revolutionary new mowing machine invented by Mr Budding in 1829 – set off the vivid carpet bedding. The effect is charmingly described by Molly, the heroine of Mrs Gaskell's *Wives and Daughters* (1864), when she visits her aristocratic neighbours at 'the Towers' and is delighted by the sight of 'green velvet lawns, bathed in sunshine … and flower beds too, scarlet, crimson, blue and orange; masses of blossom lying on the greensward'. In the book Molly helps her father's gardener to plan some new flowerbeds, pegging them out in squares using Mrs Loudon's method. The old man is quite perplexed at first, but after some explanation declares, 'All right, Miss Molly, I'se getten it in my head as clear as patchwork now'.

One of the most striking effects in Berlin woolwork was achieved using plush stitch to make a chosen motif stand out from the ground. Soft-textured flowers, fruit and birds

Elaborate carpet bedding illustrated in The Gardeners' Chronicle, *1870. The inflated effect was echoed in the curvaceous flowers in plush stitch*

Below *Roses from a typical Berlin pattern*

could be clipped into dome-like shapes, rounded like the fashionable crinolines, the flowerbeds in the garden and the swelling curves of the great greenhouses where the bedding plants were grown. Their garden counterparts were round 'pincushion' beds, with a central standard rose rising from a domed-up island of bedding plants, and 'panel planting' where groups of flowers were 'slightly elevated above the groundwork'. In *The Handy Book of the Flower Garden*, David Thomson described the effect in the gardens at Cleveland House in Clapham, where 60,000 foliage plants were used in schemes where the colouring combined 'brilliancy' with chasteness. 'In planting and finish' they were perfect; as in Berlin woolwork, 'mathematical precision' was 'the very essence of this decoration'.

GARDENING WITH SILK AND GOLD THREAD

Unlike most of his contemporaries, William Morris turned his back on the strident colours and mathematical precision of both massed bedding and Berlin woolwork. Speaking in a lecture on 'The Lesser Arts of Life' in 1882 he referred to carpet bedding as 'an aberration of the human mind', and went on, 'need I explain further? I had rather not, for when I think of it, even when I am quite alone, I blush with shame at the thought'. He likewise detested the harsh colours of the aniline dyes used in Berlin wools and the rigid precision of the canvas grid, so alien to his own free-flowing designs.

Morris found his ideal garden in the 'lovely pleasance, set with flowers, foursquare' of medieval and Tudor days. It was redolent with romantic associations, and he described it in his novels and poetry, re-creating it in his own gardens and in his embroidery and furnishing designs. He drew inspiration from happy boyhood memories of rambling and birdwatching in Epping Forest, one day discovering Queen Elizabeth's Hunting Lodge at Chigwell, where the upper room was 'hung with faded greenery' – old tapestries which transformed it with spellbinding

'Unmistakable suggestions of gardens' in the bed hangings designed by May, William Morris's daughter, c.1893, for the four-poster bed at Kelmscott Manor. Embroidered in soft but glowing crewel wools with roses entwined on trellis, the hangings evoke the carpenter's work of earlier pleasances, which Morris re-created at Kelmscott – 'well fenced from the outer world'

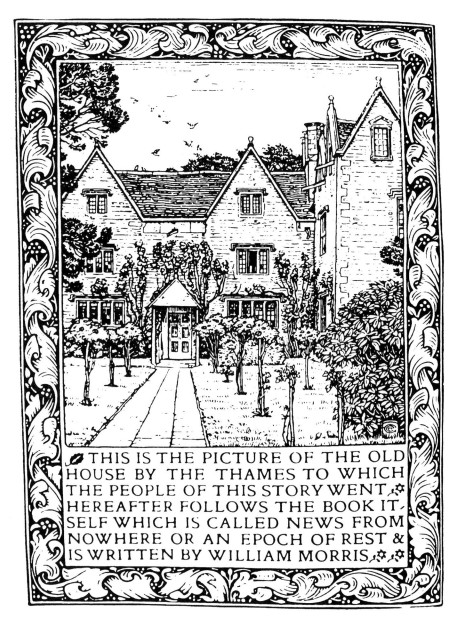

The frontispiece of William Morris's News from Nowhere *depicts the east front of Kelmscott Manor with its 'orderly' garden drawn by Charles March Gere. The novel was printed at the Kelmscott Press in 1892 and Morris designed the borders, type and ornaments*

Willow, daisy, wood sorrel and violet from Gerard's Herball. *Morris found the decorative treatment of certain plants in the old herbals suggestive of patterns*

effect. The 'impression of romance' that it made on him came back whenever he read Sir Walter Scott's description of the mysterious Green Chamber at Monkbarns in *The Antiquary*. The room was hung with Flemish tapestries depicting hunting scenes in a forest with branches covered with birds. Borders embroidered with lines from Chaucer had been added, and the bed hangings and chairs were also embroidered in dark and fading greens matching those of the tapestries. In the flickering light of a dying fire 'the tapestry waved wildly on the wall, till its dusky forms seemed to become animated', and the scene appeared to come alive before the hero's eyes. A glance at the Franklyn hanging on page 16 suggests what an impact such an experience might have on the emotions, and the passage lingered in Morris's imagination – as it must in that of anyone who reads it.

Years later, in 'The Lesser Arts of Life' lecture, Morris recalled the impact these real and imaginary rooms had made on him, and he encouraged his audience to turn their 'chamber walls into the green woods of the leafy month of June, populous of bird and beast; or a summer garden with a man and maid playing round a fountain'. This transformation he assured them 'was surely worth the trouble of doing, and the money that had to be paid for it…yes, that was more than upholstery, believe me'.

As in the past, embroidery had brought the garden indoors, and it may perhaps have been memories of the Green Chamber that suggested the decoration of the dining room at Red House, Morris's first home at Bexley Heath. Here a series of hangings was to depict Chaucer's 'Illustrious Women', with the graceful figures linked by a belt of flowers running between their feet, as if they were standing on the raised border of a medieval pleasance. If the series had been completed (only three were actually worked) the effect would surely have been that of a mysterious garden peopled with legendary figures.

Medieval and Tudor inspiration also lay behind the real garden at Red House: 'In front of the house it was spaced formally into four little square gardens making a big square altogether; each of the smaller squares had a wattled fence round it with an opening by which one entered, and all over the fence roses grew thickly.' Morris would have seen fences of this kind, and similar enclosures where the grass was powdered with flowers, in the illuminated manuscripts he collected, and his first attempt at embroidery – hangings for the bedroom at Red House – was to work simple flowers on indigo-dyed serge, spacing them on the ground in the manner of a flowery mead.

Morris taught his wife Jane some basic stitches, and together they studied the embroidery of the past, unpicking old pieces to discover forgotten techniques. He drew inspiration from the herbals, especially John Gerard's, which he had loved and perused since childhood, delighting in the illustrations and descriptions of the plants' properties. Some were recommended for dyeing, and during the 1870s he began to experiment in the

Romantically framed in honeysuckle, Jane Morris posed for Dante Gabriel Rossetti in The Day Dream. *His painting inspired this embroidered version worked by Catherine Sarah Ward c.1890*

art, gradually achieving wonderfully soft but glowing colours – unique amethysts, golds and greens – as far removed from the strident aniline dyes as it is possible to imagine. It must surely have pleased him to think of the tinctures of flowers being used to preserve their beauty in needlework.

The profusion of flowers at Kelmscott near Lechlade, which became his country home in 1871, was a constant source of pleasure and excitement, and Morris's letters reveal how closely he studied the individual plants, anticipating their beauty in bud and revelling in their expansion. He considered that the garden 'should look both orderly and rich. It should be well fenced from the outside world. It should by no means imitate either the wilfulness or the wildness of nature but should be like a

thing never to be seen except near a house'. Within the orderly framework of the garden, informal planting was the most desirable, with 'flowers that are free and interesting in their growth, leaving nature to do the desired complexity'. The structure of individual plants, rising, expanding and unfurling, fascinated him and inspired his great swirling designs.

Some of his contemporaries found their sheer exuberance overpowering. Lady Marion Alford, writing in *Needlework as Art* in 1886, described Morris's 'repetition of vegetable forms' as being like a 'vegetable garden in a tornado'. Repose was the quality she valued most in decoration, and Morris's designs were altogether too *mouvementé* for her taste. But it is this liveliness, based on a complete understanding and appreciation of natural growth and an instinctive feeling for design, that has ensured their continuing popularity. In embroidery the *mouvementé* effect was intensified by the play of light on lustrous silks and crewel wools worked on linen in free-flowing stitches – darning, long and short and stem – which followed the curves of stems, leaves and petals, capturing the essence of spring and summer.

Morris's intimate knowledge of the *craft* as well as the art of needlework, his intuitive feeling for flowers and gardens and his awareness of the links between them, comes over most expressively in a lecture he gave in 1881 entitled 'Hints on Pattern Designing': 'It is a quite delightful idea to cover a piece of linen cloth with roses, jonquils and tulips done quite natural with the needle, and we can't go too far in that direction if we only remember the nature of our craft in general: these demand that our roses and the like, however unmistakably roses, shall be quaint and naive to the last degree, and also that since we are using specially beautiful materials, that we shall make the most of them, and not forget that we are gardening with silk and gold thread.'

ART NEEDLEWORK AND THE WILD GARDEN

Morris was not alone in his dislike of massed bedding. On a freezing night in the winter of 1861, a young gardener named William Robinson let the fires in his employer's greenhouses go out, opened all the windows and exposed to the frost the entire collection of tropical plants which had been entrusted to him. He then packed his bags and left. Robinson had a hot temper, and his callous action was probably the result of an argument with the head gardener or his employer, but it also summed up feelings he was later to express in his books about the 'repulsively gaudy manner' in which vast quantities of greenhouse plants were used in bedding schemes.

Robinson's next job was far more to his taste. He was put in charge of a garden of English wild flowers in the Royal Botanical Society's garden in Regent's Park. He went on trips in search of new flowers for the collection,

Opposite *Detail of an anemone screen panel worked by Mrs Battye c.1885. Morris's designs for vigorous plants surging up through a network of smaller subsidiary flowers appear to be following Robinson's rule 'never to show the naked earth but to carpet it with dwarf subjects, then allow the taller ones to rise in their own wild way through the turf'*

'Rose Bush' and 'Rose Wreath' designs for cushions or fire screens from Morris and Co. The patterns were supplied with the design marked out on the linen, together with silks or wools

and came to appreciate the beauty of hardy plants in their natural surroundings. Gradually he evolved the idea of a 'wild garden' as an alternative to the regimented effects of massed bedding. He described how to make a 'charming little hardy garden, or a series of beds filled with the better kinds of our native plants and shrubs' in *The Wild Garden, or our Groves and Shrubberies Made Beautiful*, published in 1870. The book was well timed, for many people were beginning to tire of the geometrical gardens with their garish colours, and 'some are looking back with regret, to the old mixed border gardens with their sweet old border flowers'. These flowers, and many wild ones too, were listed by Robinson, and they included lilies, bluebells, foxgloves, columbines, honeysuckle, daffodils, irises, wild roses, even brambles.

The list corresponds exactly with the flowers coming into favour in Art Needlework, suggesting that embroiderers were as tired of Berlin woolwork as gardeners were with massed bedding. 'We can no longer be satisfied with filling up little squares or diamonds ready traced in certain fixed colours on canvas', wrote Elizabeth Glaister in *Art Embroidery*, criticizing the mechanical copying and 'gaudy obtrusiveness of the Berlin flower groups'. Her readers had only to take the Berlin wools out into a sunlit garden and compare their discordant hues with the tones of real flowers to appreciate how far removed they were from the silks and crewels of Art Needlework, which reflected the colour harmonies of nature. The pioneer of this new style of needlework was, of course, William Morris, whose designs had been available from his decorating firm,

Morris, Marshall, Faulkener and Co., since its opening in 1861, and from the Royal School of Art Needlework founded in 1872.

Like William Robinson searching out old varieties in undisturbed cottage gardens, enthusiasts of Art Needlework looked back to the embroidery of the past with renewed interest. At the Royal School, old embroideries were studied, repaired and copied as patterns. The designs could be embroidered in outline in crewel wool or silk on linen, or filled in with long and short or darning stitches. The flowers of the wild garden were especially popular, powdering the ground in 'the meadow effect' advocated by Robinson, or spaced in simple borders like those he described in his most popular book, *The English Flower Garden* (1883). 'The simplest flowers are the best,' advised Mrs Glaister, 'as they are those which can most fully be expressed by the fewest lines, if in outline, and with the fewest shades of colour. It will be obvious that double flowers are unsuitable; we must be content with wild roses...and old fashioned flowers.'

In practice the wild garden needed to be as carefully planned as a Morris design. Without considerable thought, attempts at wild gardening often resulted in a rather piecemeal collection of hardy plants, just as, in Mrs Glaister's admonitory phrase, a profusion of Art Needlework flowers 'on pieces of linen hung over the furniture' merely recalled 'a washing day'. A flood of poor-quality imitations of 'Morris' designs inadequately worked in the drab 'art' colours was threatening to engulf the domestic interior. Wild flowers quickly became a cliché, with periwinkles, dog roses and honeysuckle ramping over cushions, fire screens and covers as profusely as over the trellis of the 'old-fashioned' garden.

JAPONAISERIE

Tiring of these wishy-washy effects, some embroiderers looked with interest at the gorgeous Japanese embroideries exquisitely worked with cranes and chrysanthemums in lustrous silks and gold displayed at Liberty's in Regent Street and in the Exhibition Room at the Royal School of Art Needlework. It was tempting to imagine that they could emulate these wonderful creations, and they quickly took advantage of the 'japonaiserie' designs rushed out by commercial firms. Elizabeth Glaister described the kind of patterns available for screens in her most popular book, *Needlework*, published in 1880: 'Each panel is a kind of picture. The more solid plants grow up from the ground, or out of very conventional water; higher up a bird flies across, or perches, and is balanced by a suggestion of a cloud or a projecting spray of flowers.'

As had happened when chinoiserie became popular in the late seventeenth century, the 'most obvious and superficial qualities' of Japanese art were seized on by embroiderers and other artists and craftsmen. The complex symbolism of Japanese flowers and gardens remained a mystery to most people, and, as Elizabeth Glaister emphasized in *Art Embroidery*, 'the beauties of Japanese Needlework are, like those of other art work from that wonderful land very far from being rightly understood here by more than a few'. One designer who appreciated the 'real merit' of Japanese art work was Thomas Jeckyll. His wall hanging of cranes and a garden pagoda in cast iron, designed for two important exhibitions in the 1870s, the first at Philadelphia and the second in Paris, attracted much attention. The birds and their setting of flowers and foliage were worked to show off the structure of feathers and leaves, and in this they were

Detail of a wall hanging by Thomas Jeckyll in silks and wool on cotton sheeting

Bronze cranes and stone lanterns by a water-lily tank in V. N. Gauntlett's nursery, illustrated in the 1901 catalogue. 'This blending of East and West will make for daintiness and simplicity in the garden,' enthused a writer in The Gardener's Magazine *(quoted at length in the catalogue), captivated by the mystic 'spell that has touched the quiet slumbering beauty of the Old English Garden'*

Below Stone lanterns and stepping stones in the garden of Jizo-In, Mibu from Josiah Conder's Landscape Gardening in Japan, *1893*

faithful to Japanese technique, whose 'fineness, firmness and precision of workmanship' Walter Crane so much admired.

As adapted by Western designers japonaiserie patterns were most effective on large-scale hangings and screens, but for amateurs in search of novelty, motifs for decorating less ambitious furnishings including irregular-shaped pieces in crazy patchwork were the most popular. Perhaps William Morris had such items particularly in mind when he wrote an article in the catalogue of the first Arts and Crafts Exhibition in London in 1888, warning enthusiasts against 'the feeble imitations of Japanese art that are so disastrously common among us. The Japanese are admirable naturalists, wonderful skilful draughtsmen, deft beyond all others in mere execution of whatever they take in hand…But with all this a Japanese design is absolutely worthless unless it is executed with Japanese skill'.

It was advice that embroiderers and gardeners seldom took sufficiently to heart, though their attempts to re-create the 'mystic spell of that flowery land' continued well into the twentieth century. They found inspiration in real gardens like the one laid out in miniature by a Japanese landscape gardener at Alexandra Palace, in books like Joseph Conder's *Landscape Gardening in Japan*, and in the catalogues put out by V. N. Gauntlett and Company, who specialized in the design and laying out of Japanese gardens and offered a seductive range of 'special items' – Japanese maples 'to light up the whole landscape', magnolias, cherries and azaleas, together with 'the Japanese Ideal in Stonework' in the shape of 'interesting old Stone seats, exquisite Stone Bridges and charming Stone Lanterns which at nightfall shed their diffused rays over rippling pools and bridges'.

CHAPTER 6

Twentieth-Century Gardens

'The best purpose of a garden is to give delight and to give refreshment of mind'
GERTRUDE JEKYLL, *WALL AND WATER GARDENS*, 1901

THE INFLUENCE OF MISS JEKYLL

A deep involvement in plants, garden design and embroidery make Gertrude Jekyll (1843–1932) the perfect companion to lead us into the twentieth century. The ideal of the artist-craftsman appealed to her strongly and, like William Morris, whom she met in 1869, she combined talent for design with practical experience of the many crafts that interested her. To her deep disappointment, the increasing short-sightedness that had troubled her since childhood cut her off from painting and embroidery during her forties, and it was then that she redirected her creative talents to garden design and writing.

In the realm of garden design she has been lastingly influential and a number of her gardens have been lovingly restored. Her many books and articles remain an inspiration and a delight to read, and they hold a particular fascination for those who share a dual interest in gardens and embroidery, as many of her remarks on gardens and plant associations, especially concerning colour and design, are equally apt when applied to needlework.

In *Home and Garden*, published in 1900, she wrote about the interior of Munstead Wood, the house designed for her by her friend and associate, the young Edwin Lutyens, and her love of needlework comes out strongly in the description of her home. On her travels abroad she collected embroideries of all kinds, both old and new. Some were displayed in the house, while most were preserved in 'handy dark green boxes in deep panelled cupboards', together with her own materials – Algerian and other embroidery silks, crewel wools, chenille and coloured cottons and linens, as well as silks and cottons for working on.

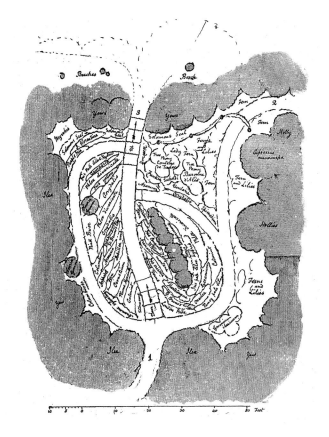

The plan of Miss Jekyll's 'Hidden Garden' at Munstead Wood from Colour Schemes for the Flower Garden. *Designed in a restricted scheme of 'tenderer tones' for late-spring enjoyment and enclosed with dark yews and* hollies, this was a secret place planted with drifts of hostas, corydalis and columbines whose pale purplish blooms reminded her of 'an old much-washed cotton patchwork quilt' – a hint for a modern interpretation, perhaps?

Miss Jekyll is framed in an arch ingeniously incorporating her border plans in Sonja Head's witty Sketches from the Life of Miss Jekyll, *1994. Edwin Lutyens'* affectionately humorous drawings form an outer frame, together with examples of her own well-drawn designs. Hand embroidery on evenweave linen, 1994

Miss Jekyll's influence can be seen in Mrs Berners Wilson's embroidery of a water garden worked in coloured silks, c.1930. This 'plant picture…seen from the opposite side of the stream' features exactly the kind of 'good grouping' of iris and water plants advocated in Miss Jekyll's chapter on 'The Streamside Garden' in Wall and Water Gardens

'From time to time many of the materials came into use, while the rest are for the pleasure of turning over myself and showing to friends of like tastes, and about it all is the comfortable feeling that everything is kept clean and safe and easily accessible.' Her words suggest that she was on the same closely intimate and friendly terms with the materials of embroidery as she was with the plants she loved. Her cupboards, made with the same loving craftsmanship as everything else in the house, recall John Rea's seventeenth-century 'cabinet' garden (see page 55) with its precious contents.

Sadly, few of Gertrude Jekyll's embroideries have survived, but they were obviously beautiful both in design and technique, so much so that they attracted Lord Leighton's attention when she first exhibited some furnishings at the London International Exhibition in New Bond Street in 1870. He immediately commissioned a table cover in a similar 'rich tone' for his dining room at Leighton House, and soon after she was busy on a set of six flower and berry cushions for another painter, her friend Hercules Brabazon. Fortunately she kept at least two of the designs – the iris and periwinkle – which were later included in a *Handbook of Embroidery* published by the Royal School of Art Needlework in 1880.

Miss Jekyll's garden designs featured elongated groupings of plants most carefully planned to interweave and 'form beautiful pictures'. She believed it essential to 'place every plant or group of plants with such thoughtful care and attention that they shall form part of a harmonious whole, and that successive portions, or in some cases even single details, shall show series of pictures'. This extract is taken from *Colour Schemes for the Garden*, which of all her books is the most enlightening and stimulating for embroiderers. She shared William Robinson's deep love of plants but she had a surer understanding of how best to use them to create beautiful pictures, and she warned her readers of the pitfalls of 'natural' gardening. Ill-assorted plants in the garden were no better than dabs of paint set out on a palette, or a library 'made up of single volumes when there should be complete sets. Given the same space of ground and the same materials they may be fashioned either into a dream of beauty, a place of perfect rest and refreshment of minds…or they may be so misused that everything is jarring and displeasing'.

Jarring effects were most likely to result when too many plants were used, and Miss Jekyll warned against the temptation of acquiring plants without a clear idea of how they were to be arranged. Her borders were famous for their profusion, but this effect was achieved by rigorous restraint in the choice of each plant to enhance the textures, tones and shapes of its neighbours. Her groups were always generous, thus avoiding the 'shopwindow' or 'washing day' effect which led the plantsman E. A. Bowles to criticize the 'school of gardening that encourages the selection of plants merely as artistic furniture chosen for colour only, like ribbons or embroidery silk'.

Miss Jekyll's designs of periwinkle and iris were illustrated in the Handbook *of Embroidery, published by the Royal School of Art Needlework in 1880*

Colour was of crucial importance, and her use of it made her gardens unique; but Miss Jekyll was equally concerned with the setting, the various qualities of the plants involved and how best to make them work together to realize the effect she had in mind. One imagines her as a young woman, assembling her embroidery materials and considering the role they were to play in the whole design, which would be as far removed from mere 'artistic furniture' as her sensitive garden pictures.

As a young woman she had enrolled at the South Kensington School of Art, where she attended lectures on colour theory and studied books on the subject. She continued to refine her sense of colour throughout her life, calling it a kind of 'optical gastronomy' – food for the eye in which each course is so designed that it is the best possible preparation for the ones to come. This gastronomy is best appreciated in 'Gardens of Special Colouring', in which a particular colour predominates –

blue, grey, gold and green, the forerunners of the white and silver gardens of the later twentieth century – or patios where foliage plants make refreshing green pictures within a small compass. As always, Miss Jekyll combined common sense with artistic knowledge and a sense of beauty, and she reminded her readers that including flowers just because they were 'grey' or 'blue' was not the only criterion. 'Any experienced colourist knows that the blues will be more telling – more purely blue – by the rightly placed complementary colour.'

Knowing where to place the right shade of the complementary colour, and how much to use, comes only with long experience, and Gertrude Jekyll never minimized the difficulties. She spent half her life contriving ways of achieving beauty and harmony in the garden, but when she looked back, she could remember no part of all this that was not full of pleasure and encouragement: 'For the love of gardening is a seed that once sown never dies, but always grows and grows to an enduring and ever increasing source of happiness.'

CHILDREN AND GARDENS

The seed was sown early in Miss Jekyll's own childhood, as she tells us in *Children and Gardens* (1911), the most endearingly personal of all her books. It was written at Edwin Lutyens' suggestion to foster the love of gardening in children, and it imparts practical advice with enthusiasm and the most engaging humour. Here she is introducing herself in the opening chapter: 'Well do I remember the time when I thought there were two kinds of people in the world – children and grown ups – and that the world really belonged to children. And I think it is because I have been more or less a child all my life, that I still feel like a child in many ways although from the number of years I have lived I ought to know that I am quite an old woman.' She was 65 at the time. She looks back to her own childhood and tells how she made daisy chains in Berkeley Square and was 'attracted by dandelions' in Green Park. She and her sister had adjoining gardens with box-edged borders, laid out between the shrubbery

Opposite, left 'The Old Playhouse' from Miss Jekyll's Children and Gardens. *The idea of a book to encourage young gardeners was suggested to her by Edwin Lutyens. The 'pretty lady' is Elizabeth von Arnim, author of* Elizabeth and her German Garden, *photographed by Ellen Willmott, the celebrated plantswoman*

Opposite, right *Gerard Brender à Brandis brings out the decorative quality of the dandelion in this wood engraving from* Portraits of Flowers. *His treatment suggests inlay with surface stitchery*

Above *Like Miss Jekyll, Jennifer Wilson was 'attracted by dandelions'. Inspired by their curious names, she worked their distinctive shapes on hand-dyed felt, 1994*

of her parents' garden and a field. She wanted children to have a playhouse in the garden, and she illustrates this idea with a plan and a photograph of a 'pretty lady' sitting outside a playhouse 'trying to think herself a child again'.

Her words bring to mind two embroideries of children picking flowers, happy and absorbed in a world of their own, recalling the enchanted atmosphere of Frances Hodgson Burnett's *The Secret Garden*, published in 1911, the same year as Jekyll's *Children and Gardens*. May Kuck's roundel draws inspiration from the flowery mead of the millefleur tapestries, and Mary Newill's panel, embroidered around 1900 when she was teaching embroidery at the Birmingham School of Art, evokes the 'olde fashioned'

pleasance that gardeners inspired by William Morris had been busily re-creating since his day. With its feeling of enclosure and jumble of woodland and border flowers, Mary Newill's panel is close to the dream-like spirit of *The Secret Garden*: 'I wouldn't want it to look like a gardener's garden, all clipped and spick an' span, would you?' says the country boy Dickon to Mary, the heroine of the story. Miss Jekyll would have agreed, declaring herself 'perpetually at war with the gardener for over trimmers'.

She liked profusion and natural-looking effects in the planting, controlled by a skilful yet unobtrusive plan. The garden she enjoyed as a child had yew hedges, frontiers of a private land, like the scene in *Spring*, worked in about 1910, where a girl is picking blossom. It recalls the gardens depicted by Walter Crane and Kate Greenaway in their books for children, and perhaps one of these artists inspired Katherine Powell's exquisitely worked hand screen 'Mary Mary Quite Contrary' (see page 128) with its topiary-topped hedge and cockleshell borders. Hedged enclosures enlivened with, decorative orchards, fanciful topiary old-fashioned flowers, sundials and 'Shakespeare' borders featuring plants named in his plays were favourite elements in the small-scale intimate gardens of many Arts and Crafts houses. They reflect a nostalgia for the past seen also in the lasting vogue for the cottage garden, epitomized in a machine-embroidered picture copied, in Singer's 'artistic' workroom, from one of the many Victorian and Edwardian watercolours idealizing a rural idyll that existed more in the artist's imagination than in reality.

Opposite *The special atmosphere of secluded gardens so magically evoked in* The Secret Garden *is echoed in Mary Newill's panel, where fruit trees and a picket fence enclose the children's small plot. Wools on linen in chain, split, and long and short stitches*

Roundel of a girl picking flowers worked in tent stitch by May Kuck, c.1910. Interviewed about her design sources in The Embroideress, *she replied, 'As I walk down a lane or in a garden, I suddenly see the whole thing complete in needlework.' She always*

began by making a 'very careful coloured drawing exactly to scale', which she would transfer by holding the canvas over the paper against the light

'My Lady's Garden', an
illustration by Walter Crane for
The Baby's Opera, 1877

The ingenious use of laid and
shadow work make
Katherine Powell's hand
screen 'Mary, Mary Quite
Contrary' (c.1910) as perfect
on the back as it is on the
front. Worked with darning,
stem and satin stitches, it is
set in a silver frame

Appliqué and simple
stitchery in Spring, c.1910

The real and topiary peacocks, the hedged enclosure and armillary sphere combine to create a mysterious romantic atmosphere evocative of earlier pleasances in this drawing of 'A Garden Enclosed' by W. R. Lethaby in J. D. Sedding's Gardencraft Old and New, *1891*

Poster of an embroidery worked in Singer's workrooms to advertise the 'artistic' use of their sewing machines. The cottage cult was also reflected in countless fire screens depicting crinoline ladies by hollyhock borders, worked from transfers in the 1920s and 1930s

Cottage garden illustrated in William Robinson's The English Flower Garden. *'Nothing is prettier than an English cottage garden,' he wrote, extolling the charm of natural planting in simple plots*

PARTLY FORMAL, PARTLY CONTROLLED WILD

In *Old West Surrey* (1904) Miss Jekyll praised 'the little cottage gardens that help to make our English waysides the prettiest in the world'. On her travels round the countryside she found much to interest her in cottage-garden plants 'growing beautifully together by some happy chance', some of which provided ideas for her own garden, Munstead Wood, near Godalming in Surrey. Visiting her there around 1900, the architect Harold Falkner described the garden as 'partly formal, partly controlled wild', a perceptive phrase which aptly sums up a style of gardening that has remained popular throughout the century, bringing countless visitors to enjoy such celebrated gardens as Hidcote, Sissinghurst and Great Dixter. The formula is simple, and appeals as much to embroiderers as to gardeners: once an underlying order is established, enthusiasts can experiment with texture, tone and form, making imaginative use of the wealth of plants, material and threads now available. Vita Sackville-West described Hidcote, laid out by Lawrence Johnston from 1907, as 'a cottage garden on a glorified scale... or rather a series of cottage gardens, in so far as the plants grow in a jumble...' The key difference was that in real cottage gardens the charming effect was most often accidental rather than planned, whereas at Hidcote it was orchestrated with great sophistication and skill. The

luxuriant planting and perfectly proportioned hedges combined to give the 'illusion of enclosure' Vita Sackville-West loved and was to re-create with such spellbinding effect in her own garden at Sissinghurst, begun in 1930.

Sissinghurst has become a mecca for embroiderers just as much as for gardeners. Some of us are drawn by the uniquely seductive harmonies and contrasts of flowers, shrubs and bulbs, and by the enticingly framed views through archways in walls and gaps in hedges, any one of which might offer an exciting starting-point for needle-work. Others are inspired by the views from the central tower which reveal the strong lines of Harold Nicolson's underlying plan, the perfect framework for his wife's exuberant planting. Looking down on the enclosures from the tower is rather like lifting the roof from a doll's house to reveal the rooms inside. We glimpse their individual character, with the happy anticipation of descending to explore their contents at leisure, one by one.

The Sissinghurst plan looks back to the compartments of the Elizabethan garden and Sir William Temple's ideal arrangement of 'rooms out of which you step into another'. It has influenced many designers, and indeed the 'garden room', the knot and the cottage garden have become favourite models, adopted and adapted by gardeners and embroiderers alike. The needlework version often takes the shape of a box which preserves the 'illusion of enclosure' until the lid is lifted to reveal 'a miniature surprise'. The

Opposite The closely planted borders in Juliet Wheeler's garden continue the cottage cult in their profusion. Her skilful collage emphasizes the flower shapes, and the choice of fabrics conveys the texture of walls and flagstones

The smaller scale of modern gardens is charmingly illustrated in Evelyn Dunbar and Cyril Mahoney's Gardener's Choice *(1937). 'Nowadays gardens generally serve as an extension to the house,' they wrote, and their 'Design for a Country or Suburban*

Garden' was above all 'simple and adaptable', *a quiet setting for the plant inhabitants described in their book. It is a type of plan that has inspired a number of 'secret' embroidered gardens ingeniously enclosed within the walls of a box*

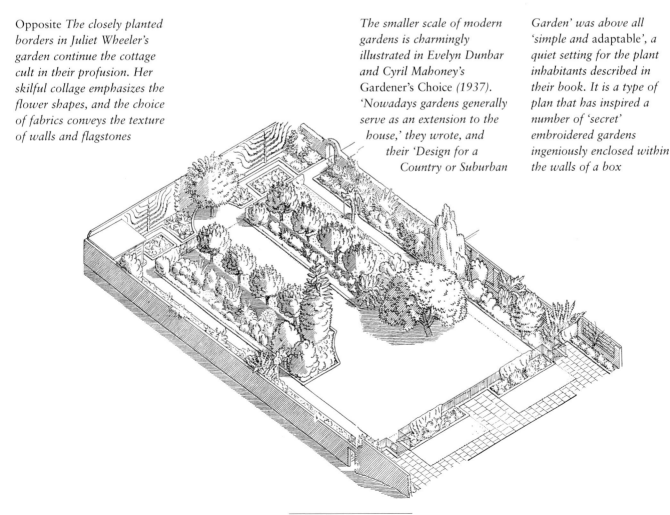

Opposite *The couplet 'Into your garden you can walk and with the plants and flowers talk' stitched round the lid of Beppy Berlin's ingenious box (1995) (above right) hints at the interior 'surprise' – when the lid is removed, the sides fall open to reveal Grandma enjoying her garden (above left). The sides and top are stitched with flower motifs in crewelwork*

Below left *The patterns displayed inside one of Beppy Berlin's knot boxes (the other is shown closed) are backstitched, with the flowers and topiary bird in French knots. Jo Balkwill's 'Beehive' box (below right) contains a tiny pool garden. Mazes ornament the lids, and knot patterns the sides of all three boxes, which are worked with counted thread on evenweave cotton*

The 'strong lines' of Jan Attril's canvaswork garden plan provide a satisfying framework for 'planting' with texture and colour

phrase ends a passage in the 'Summer' section of Vita Sackville-West's poem 'The Garden' (1946) in which she describes the delights and challenges of gardening through the seasons. Embroiderers as well as gardeners should heed her words when she asserts her firm belief that 'gardens should be romantic, but severe'. A plan with 'strong lines' is the first essential in both embroidery and garden design, whatever the size of the project.

Hidcote and Sissinghurst were laid out on a scale which is rarely attempted today. Since the 1930s gardens have generally been far less extensive, but though space, time and labour are more restricted than ever before, the interest and pleasure in gardens is undiminished. The idea expressed over three centuries ago by the herbalist William Coles that 'a house though otherwise beautiful, if it hath no garden belonging to it is more like a prison than a house' is now even truer, when the garden provides repose and relaxation as an antidote to the pressures and stress of modern life. Here, as in embroidery, we can become absorbed in a private world, working at our own pace on what pleases us most. The day-by-day experience of the real garden – pricking out seedlings, pruning, planning

improvements in the border, watering with a sprinkler – generates a succession of new ideas for stitchery, as we may see in the work of Jenny Chippindale, Anne Kinniment, Julia Barton, Dr Jim Smart, to name but a few whose embroidery is paralleled by their skill and success in garden-making.

Anne Kinniment's garden is a wildlife haven in Northumberland, one of a group of gardens tended by keen plantsmen and women in the village of Kirkwhelpington, which open together for the National Gardens Scheme. Her sensitive embroideries evoke the meadow gardening in her own and some of her neighbours' gardens. Concern for ecology and conserving wild flowers together with the informal charm of this type of gardening have made it increasingly popular, and it is no surprise to find that the vogue is reflected in embroidery. But it is a mistake to assume that either wild or meadow gardening is an easy option in practical terms. The renowned alpine collector Reginald Farrer called the wild garden 'the very worst and most extravagant of frauds, requiring a supervision no less incessant and close than in any parterre or border'; Mrs Earle found it 'a delusion and a snare', and Miss Jekyll reflected that 'of all kinds of planting, wild gardening needs the greatest caution and restraint'. Restraint was a favourite word of hers – she once called gardening *l'art des sacrifices* – but without it the wild or meadow garden can easily become merely messy and incoherent. The problem is that it *looks* easy, both in the real garden and in needlework, seducing us into believing

Anne Kinniment records the 'semi-wild' part of her garden merging into woodland at Kirkwhelpington. Grasses mingle with cow parsley and buttercups worked in hand and machine embroidery on a painted ground

Opposite *Jenny Chippindale's embroidery records favourite plants in her garden in Northamptonshire. Her scarlet oriental poppies are made from pleated silk chiffon*

that beautiful effects can be achieved with the minimum of preparation and effort. The embroiderer does not have to worry about rampant grasses smothering more fragile subjects, but must be rigorously selective in choosing plants that will transpose and group well in stitchery. Anne Kinniment's needlework skill and her close and constant observation of the plants she loves gives her an intuitive feeling for rendering the natural rhythms of stems swaying in the breeze, tendrils interweaving, petals and seeds falling and scattering.

Her delicate treatment makes an interesting contrast to Jenny Chippindale's wonderfully bold and exuberant poppies. Colours of this intensity are difficult to place in the garden, particularly if space is limited. Miss Jekyll admired the richest and most vibrant reds and purples 'culminating into gorgeousness' as a central crescendo in her famous colour-graded borders, and visitors to Sissinghurst have gasped at the unexpected brilliance as they enter the sunset garden, but in general bright, strong reds and oranges

Roy and Barbara Hirst's
Acanthus Invasion *records
Roy's attempts to curb the
take-over of the plant
introduced for architectural
effect in his garden. The
gardener was made by
Barbara in raised work, and
Roy worked the three-
dimensional leaves and flower
spikes in machine embroidery
on vanishing muslin*

*Inspired by the famous
potager at Barnsley House,
Sue Rangeley's screen (1997)
records poppies, Welsh
onions and peas dancing over
pea sticks at high summer.
Colourful textures with
machine and hand work
against the subtle linear
graphite tones of sketched
and painted trellis, accented
with twin needled geometrics*

have been eclipsed in popularity by the opalescent harmonies of soft pinks, blues and violet. Now there is a reaction; the once-loved grey or silver garden looks insipid and out of date, and bright colours are making a comeback, presenting a whole new range of contrasts and harmonies for us to try out, if we dare. This swing of the pendulum owes much to the endlessly thought-provoking writing and gardens of Beth Chatto and Christopher Lloyd at Elmstead Market in Essex and Great Dixter in East Sussex respectively. Ever eager to experiment, Christopher Lloyd recently replanted the Rose Garden at Dixter, jubilantly rooting out the roses to create a 'jungle of luxuriance', a dazzling autumn display of cannas, dahlias, red-hot pokers and exotic foliage plants chosen for their bold leaves and vibrant colours – 'optical gastronomy' indeed, and a sure way to make you reconsider your taste!

Will needlework on garden themes reflect this trend? With notable exceptions, such as Richard Box and Kaffe Fasset, the garden enthusiast's palette has been predominantly low key, with a marked preference for subtle harmonies rather than bold contrasts. But bright colour can become addictive, jolting one out of preconceived ideas, as more and more embroiderers have found after seeing the rivers of orange nasturtiums in Monet's garden at Giverny, or the spectacular displays of ornamentally grown ruby chard, tomatoes and gourds at Villandry.

Vegetables, together with herbs and fruit, grown ornamentally in a potager or among flowers in a border, delight the eye as much as the palate, and their shapes and colours are just as tantalizing for embroiderers. The orderly layout of neat rows and squares provides a ready-made outline for inventive stitchery, and it is no surprise to find the popularity of the potager increasingly reflected in needlework. The criss-crossing of bean poles, pea sticks and wigwams of bamboo canes add diagonal interest to a design, and the striking geometry of mesh-covered fruit cages, Victorian hand lights or rhubarb-forcing jars beside a curved brick wall gives it further strength, suggesting experiments in drawn fabric or thread stitches, patchwork, inlay or raised work. Patterns and inspiring contrasts of shape, colour and texture abound (for example) in the juxtaposition of red cabbage with leeks, or statuesque artichokes with a tangle of full-podded peas; but finding exactly the appropriate stitch or method to transpose them can be tricky. Leeks suggest fish bone or elongated fly, and bold artichoke heads and leaves crewelwork, a difficult method to update, but one that could be perfect for a potager. A mosaic of various frilled lettuces appeals to one embroiderer as abstract patterning, best realized on canvas, and to another as raised work,

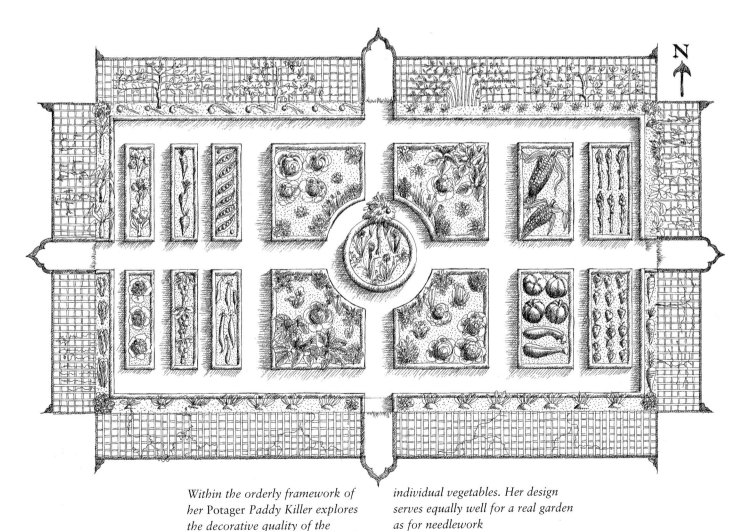

Within the orderly framework of her Potager *Paddy Killer explores the decorative quality of the individual vegetables. Her design serves equally well for a real garden as for needlework*

with each leaf rendered as realistically as possible – in detached buttonhole perhaps, or machining on vanishing muslin. Vegetable gardening challenges the embroiderer's skill and ingenuity as much as the gardener's, and the ultimate test might be to make a 'salad ball…of a marvellous form, and divers in taste', as described by Thomas Hill in 1577 in *The Gardener's Labyrinth* in which seedling lettuce, cress, basil, and rocket sprouted out from a ball of earth supported on a radish!

Another trend that may prove influential is the innovative and imaginative use of perennials and grasses in naturalistic or 'ecological' schemes, recently developed in gardens and parks on the Continent. Based on the way indigenous plants group themselves in the wild, extensive drifts or blocks are juxtaposed and repeated to create pleasingly rhythmical patterns and textural contrasts – a skilfully contrived patchwork, from a distance resembling an abstract design. The grasses and perennials most favoured in this type of planting are increasingly featured at flower shows – always instructive barometers of fashion.

Will this naturalistic style be taken up by embroiderers in search of new ideas? Grasses, for example, are marvellously diverse in their outlines – stately, plume-like, gauzy, arching in fountains – dramatic when backlit, interesting in winter, asking to be couched or stitched into handmade paper, or tried out in goldwork. Put too many together and the effect, as in the real garden, will be messy; they look best combined with more substantial plants with bold leaves or flowerheads, and are prized by the modernists – contemporary designers determined to break out of the 'romantic' time warp and to create unfussy, functional schemes in which the innovative use of the hard materials – stone, gravel, water, timber – is as important as the planting. With a firm emphasis on texture and form, their work could prove stimulating and instructive for embroiderers in search of a distinctive style that looks forward to the future rather than back to the past.

The delight of 'gardening with silk and gold thread' is that it allows us to experiment with new ideas. Like the real garden, embroidery – in the words of the Elizabethan writer Thomas Hill – is 'a ground plot for the mind', an activity that gives free rein to the imagination, and is both absorbing and deeply satisfying, soothing yet stimulating. Whatever we stitch in silk and gold, whether it is influenced by the latest trends or draws inspiration from the patterns and plants of the past, it will still reflect our pleasure in our own gardens and may survive long after those much-loved creations have gone.

Opposite Ordered profusion in the Potager at Burton Agnes Hall, hand embroidered by Janet Haigh (1966). Part of a panel depicting the New

Elizabethan Gardens designed by Susan Cunliffe-Lister. Standard bays, apples and roses add vertical interest to the layout

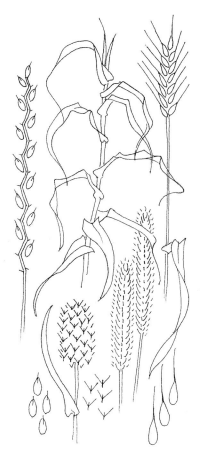

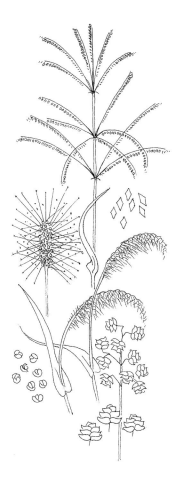

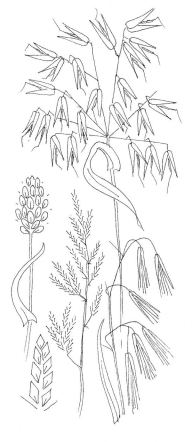

Mary Grierson's drawing of grasses emphasizes their potential for embroidery

CHAPTER 7

Ideas for Embroidering Gardens

'The whole art of designing consists in a just agreement of the several parts one with another'
STEPHEN SWITZER, *ICHNOGRAPHIA RUSTICA*, 1742

PATTERNS AND PLANS

As we have seen, many types of garden plan, knots and parterres in particular, are interchangeable with embroidery designs; others need adapting to suit the scale of the project one has in mind. Pictorial plans are especially appealing, and they are full of suggestions for stitchery. Take, for example, the early eighteenth-century plans devised by John Rocque which depict the irregular layout of the new landscape gardens, set within a framework of small-scale illustrations of the principal features. Garden visiting had become enormously popular, and by perusing

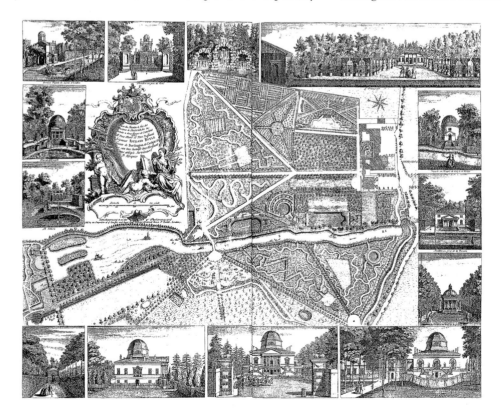

Left J*ohn Rocque's pictorial plan of the gardens at Chiswick, 1736, was the starting point for Paddy Killer's counterpane* (opposite). *The valances and pair of pillows at the head of the bed are ornamented with garden buildings after designs by Thomas Wright, Thomas Robins and Lord Burlington; the wrought-iron bedhead was inspired by the borders framing Thomas Robins' pictures*

these plans people who had heard or read about the dramatic changes in design could gain a visual impression of the garden before actually visiting it. The reality was, of course, even more exciting. 'I cannot describe Wilton,' wrote Mrs Montagu in September 1747, 'it exceeds all that poetry and painting can represent.'

When we look at a picture we are static, but to appreciate a landscape garden we must move through it. How can we recapture this particular pleasure in embroidery, and transform a visual and emotional experience into a

design? Rocque's plan shows the way, conveying movement through the paths on the main, central plan, interspersed with pauses while the visitor stops to admire the features, frozen as vignettes round the edge. His decorative presentation suggests the design of a bedspread, with a simplified plan of the garden ornamenting the surface of the bed and the features to which the paths lead embroidered round the edge and sides.

The idea could be adapted using the up-to-date plans included in most guide books, combining them with engravings or photographs of the main garden features. But on your visit you might prefer to sit and draw, or pause and take photographs to record more personal impressions as the basis of your design. Alternatively you could follow the example of the eighteenth-century artists who juxtaposed real and imaginary features in idealized landscape capriccios. The bedcover could become a capriccio of a most personal kind, a fanciful design bringing together favourite buildings and prospects – some real, some seen in books or paintings. I would one day like to embroider a set of bed furnishings inspired by the rococo gardens of Thomas Robins (see page 84). Garlands of flowers frame his enchanting views, and their embroidered counterparts would twine along the valances of the bed, their serpentine curves echoed in the paths on the coverlet and the fanciful outlines of the pavilions and follies worked in the border.

Few of the gardens Robins recorded remain, but we can still enjoy Painswick in Gloucestershire, happily restored over recent years to reassume much of its original beauty and enchantment. The features are sited within a relatively small compass and the small, intimate scale of the garden makes it an ideal starting point for embroidery, less daunting than the later, vast and apparently natural landscapes of Capability Brown. A visit to Painswick would be sure to spark the imagination – in May perhaps, when the little buildings are framed in fresh greenery, or in February, when snowdrops carpet the ground, and the plan is clearest to the eye. Robins framed one of his bird's-eye views of Painswick, painted in 1748, in a ravishingly pretty border of shells, twining vetch and lilies of the valley on a midnight blue ground – inspiration perhaps for a shell-embroidered box opening up to reveal vignettes of the garden.

PICTURES

Studying the ways in which artists and draughtsmen present gardens can provide stimulating ideas for embroidery. Of course, looking at a painting or a book illustration, however detailed, cannot replace seeing the garden with your own eyes. The artist's vision, whether it is photographically accurate or romantically idealized, puts you at one remove from the garden, but this distancing brings its own rewards. Seeing the rococo garden through Robins' eyes, for example, heightens its imaginative appeal, and at the same time suggests ways of transposing his enchanted world into embroidery. In depicting a garden, the artist must first decide on a viewpoint and scale, and embroiderers, faced with similar choices, may find that the artist's decision to exaggerate the perspective or play games with the scale sets them off on new and exciting paths.

The naïve perspective and simple symbols of William Lawson's terraced garden were the starting point for Paddy Killer's cushion designs, which ingeniously expand upon Lawson's bare proposal, and her mirror frame idea, sparked off by the title page of Parkinson's *Paradisus Terrestris*, is equally inventive in redisposing the decorative elements. It is the disproportionate scale of the plants represented in this picture of Eden – huge in comparison to the toy-like Adam and Eve, and equally out of scale one with another – that creates such a beguiling and fanciful effect. The natural phenomena appear wondrous and extraordinary – as they did to seventeenth-century eyes – and this was the effect that Janet Haigh wanted to capture and intensify in embroidery. In her *Paradisus*, the reality of the plants is heightened by rendering the colours, shapes and markings as naturalistically as possible, and by introducing disquieting newcomers – ivy-clad oaks in the

Opposite Paddy Killer wittily rearranges the decorative elements of William Lawson's pictorial plan (below) in her cushion designs, combining fountain and knot in one and mount and topiary figures in another. A pear, borrowed from a cover at Hardwick Hall, represents the orchard and a 'Kitching Garden' completes the set

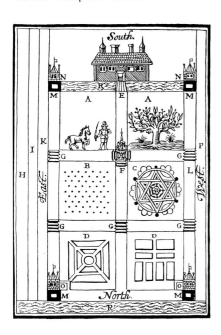

Right Paddy Killer turns the title page of the Paradisus Terrestris *inside out as a stumpwork mirror frame design, transferring the people and plants to a scalloped border round the distinctive oval shape of the glass*

Janet Haigh turns the title page of Parkinson's Eden through 90 degrees to create her own earthly paradise, retaining the decorative border of golden sun rays in the original, and the clouds and angels. The eye of heaven above is made brilliant with flowers in contrast to the ominous hell below. The emerald silk satin ground enhances the dramatic raised work of the plants, their petals each separately stitched in silks then bonded, hemmed or cut out to form the flowers. Adam and Eve and the clouds are in trapunto stuffing

shapes of a boxer and a laughing fox in the background. Not all natural phenomena are as benign as those in Parkinson's Eden, and in the foreground of this embroidered version the title cartouche becomes a living hell of convincingly life-like carnivorous plants reaching up for a dinner of Adam and Eve!

Everyone has their own idea of Eden. You may be making it in your own garden, or imagining it in stitchery as you sit at your worktable. For Robert Herring, writing in 1930, Eden was Kew Gardens, the setting for the engaging adventures of *Adam and Evelyn at Kew*, wittily

illustrated by Edward Bawden, an artist of particular interest to embroiderers on account of his wonderfully lively and imaginative use of line. In his drawings the simple shapes of plants, people and buildings at Kew are reminiscent of appliqué, and the needlework effect is emphasized by vigorous dots, dashes and looped and straight lines asking to be transposed in cretan, feather, coral and herringbone stitches. Similar effects can be seen in the charming decorations drawn by Evelyn Dunbar and Cyril Mahoney for their book *Gardener's Choice*, an anthology of forty favourite plants.

Above The Palm House at
Kew *and* Evelyn and Adam
in the gardens, *drawn by
Edward Bawden*

These vignettes from
Gardener's Choice *(1937)
suggest embroidery in
straight stitches, shadow or
Assisi work*

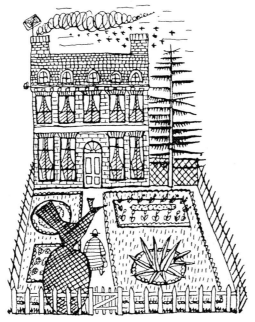

Mid-seventeenth-century beadwork picture of a lady holding three striped tulips

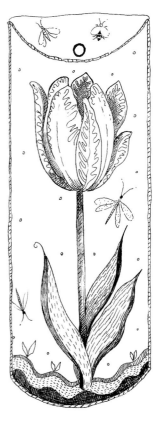

Named tulips were the stars of the garden shown in this glamorous quartet from L'Anglois' Livre de Fleurs of 1620, redrawn by Belinda Downes. Many artists depicted the blooms with attendant insects, unaware at the time that it was aphids that caused the desired variegation. Belinda adapts one of the tulips for a pen or spectacle case

PLANTS

'He is greatly in love with rare and fair flowers' wrote the herbalist John Gerard of Nicholas Lete, a fellow enthusiast and avid plant collector. Lete's passion was for carnations, but flowers, bulbs, trees, herbs and shrubs each have their devotees, and every plant can spark off a love affair and generate ideas for needlework. Plants entice the gardener just as threads lure the embroiderer. Their myriad colours, textures, and shapes delight the eye and inveigle us into purchasing them from garden centres, nurseries, flower shows and catalogues, carried away by the pleasure of acquisition. My own weakness is for tulips, and each year I find myself ordering new varieties and old favourites in the heady atmosphere of the Chelsea Flower Show tent, justifying my extravagance as 'embroidery expenses' which I shall recoup when I record them in needlework. My passion for the old varieties keeps me on a tulip trail, visiting gardens that specialize in

them, researching their history and gathering together illustrations from florilegia, the old flower books that present each variety as a star performer.

The bold shapes and eye-catching colours in seventeenth-century tulips delighted not only speculators and plant breeders, who gambled on the plain varieties breaking into arresting striped variations of colour, but also artists and craftsmen of all kinds, none more so than embroiderers. Resplendent in shimmering amber, violet and crimson beads, seductively striped in flat silk stitchery, speckled in crewelwork or with petals ingeniously raised in needlelace, they were among the favourite flowers embroidered on furnishings, pictures and cabinets. The artists who recorded the latest varieties in seventeenth-century flower books emphasized the striped, streaked and feathered markings on the petals, and these were further exaggerated by the embroiderers of those days. Modern embroiderers perusing the books now would still find them rich in suggestions for pattern-making.

The girl on the left holds her embroidery laced in a frame in this engraving by P. van de Venn from Jacob Cats' Houwelyck (Marriage) of 1625, in which the tulip is crowned with a garland of roses

Until a tulip bulb flowered no one knew if it would produce the desired markings, and excitement mounted as the moment of blooming approached. Promising tulips were often stolen, hence the Latin motto meaning 'keep it hidden while it's open' above a splendid single tulip in an ornate vase in Jacob Cats' *Howelyck* of 1625.

Perhaps it is Viceroy, one of the two most coveted and costly tulips ever sold. The astonishing number and variety of items once bartered for a single bulb inspired Janet Haigh's wonderful *Tulipomania* panel, which brings alive the excitement and folly of the craze. Here laid out for us to see are the four fat oxen, eight fat pigs, twelve fat sheep, two loads of wheat, four loads of rye, one entire bed, four barrels of beer, two barrels of butter, one thousand pounds of cheese, one suit of clothes, two hogsheads of wine and a silver beaker handed over for just one Viceroy bulb.

The elegantly cuffed hand holding up a tulip in Janet Haigh's Tulipomania *was inspired by an engraving of 'Smelling' from a set of the 'Five Senses' used in the design of the famous Mellerstain panel of 1706. The hand is in trapunto, the* cuff in tatting, and the tulips in satin stitch with a background of shaded running stitch. The stitches in the outer frame include tête de bœuf, fly, lacing and plaid stitch in gold thread on a cotton satin ground, with shisha mirrors

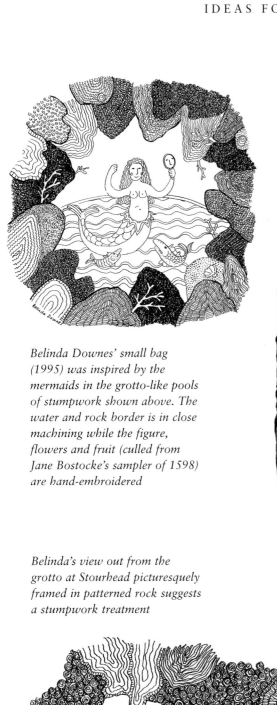

Belinda Downes' small bag (1995) was inspired by the mermaids in the grotto-like pools of stumpwork shown above. The water and rock border is in close machining while the figure, flowers and fruit (culled from Jane Bostocke's sampler of 1598) are hand-embroidered

Belinda's view out from the grotto at Stourhead picturesquely framed in patterned rock suggests a stumpwork treatment

POEMS AND PHRASES

One of the pleasures common to gardening and embroidering lies in the way our thoughts range freely and happily outwards far from the actual business of planting or weeding, of cutting out or stitching. Ideas hover in the mind, and dart about like dragonflies as we fill in background or prick out seedlings. In this daydreamy state, words and phrases become potent visual images, cross-fertilizing in the brain to suggest new projects, plant associations, patterns. Sir William Temple's strange word *Sharawadgi* (see page 83) with its overtones of wildness and irregularity becomes in my mind's eye a swathe of rough, densely stitched fabric ruched and manipulated into grotto-like forms; and swiftly following on from this, Alexander Pope's phrase 'Nymph of the Grot' (inscribed by the statue glimpsed in the gloom of the Stourhead grotto) conjures up the rocky pools of Stuart stumpwork with their attendant fish and and mermaids (see page 63), made yet more intriguing with the patterned water and encrustations of moss and shells updated in couching and machine embroidery incorporating textured and space-dyed threads undreamed of by the original makers.

Revising this book, I read and reread Andrew Marvell's hauntingly evocative poem 'The Garden', in which the last verse begins:

How well the skilful Gardener drew
Of Flowers and Herbs this Dial new;
Where from above the milder Sun
Does through a fragrant Zodiack run…

Marvell has in mind a knot laid out like an elaborate sundial, and his description set me off in pursuit of

Jennifer Wilson's Sundial *evokes Marvell's 'dial new', with a genial sun casting its rays on each flower in turn. The breeze-blowing zephyrs in the corners were inspired by seventeenth-century embroidered angels and the figures in pictorial maps. The panel is worked in machine and hand embroidery on felt made from hand-dyed fleece*

William Williams' print of the gardens at New College, Oxford, shows a dial laid out in perfectly trimmed evergreens with a metal gnomon. The knot-like layout has been updated with stylishly clipped topiary shapes

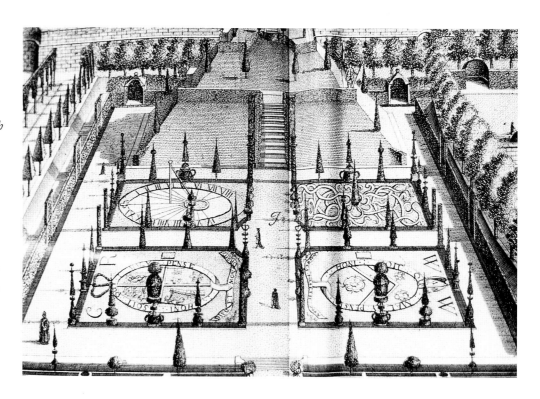

Vicki Lugg's panel records the sundial in her herb garden in Surrey. The strong outline of the octagonal dial, wrapped in space-dyed silk, makes a brilliant contrast with the profusion of herbs in delicate hand stitchery surrounding the baluster

flowery Zodiacks and sundials as starting points for embroidery. We can glimpse how Marvell's dial might have looked in William Williams' view of the garden at New College, Oxford in 1732, a rare survival from the seventeenth century, where the dial is set in a four-square plot with two coats of arms and an interlace pattern.

Sundials were popular in Tudor and Stuart gardens; they served as reliable timepieces, combining use with beauty, long before watches came into common use in the nineteenth century. They could either be laid out on the ground with living material, or free-standing, with a stone base and pedestal supporting the dial. In *The Flower Garden* (1692), William Hughes explains how to make living dials with figures cut in rosemary, thyme, hyssop and box, and this type was taken up again in Victorian 'old-fashioned' gardens. One enthusiast recommended making the dial from flowers which opened at a particular time of day, an intriguing idea, but one which would undoubtedly work better in embroidery than in the garden, where its effectiveness would be constantly threatened by the vagaries of the weather!

Sundials suggest many different treatments in embroidery. It would be fun to work a horizontal indoor dial for a table in a conservatory or garden room where there would be enough light for the gnomon – the rigid bar or style – to cast its shadow. It would need to be as flat as possible, so canvas or perhaps Assisi work might serve. Facet-headed dials might also be worth considering by those who find it satisfying to work in three dimensions.

Sundial design gives full play to the imagination. Charles II had 'many sorts of Dyalls' on the wonderful example set up in 1669 in the Privy Garden at Whitehall, one of which had painted animals in glass boxes representing the hours and another depicting royal personages. In her design, Paddy Killer represents the hours as smartly standing vegetables, with the gnomon represented by a watering can.

It is eight o'clock as the shadow from the 'watering can' gnomon falls on the cauliflower in Paddy Killer's

'TAKE ALL THE SUN GOES ROUND'. Her watercolour design was later machine-embroidered on satin

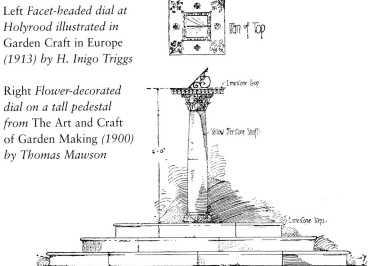

Left *Facet-headed dial at Holyrood illustrated in* Garden Craft in Europe *(1913) by H. Inigo Triggs*

Right *Flower-decorated dial on a tall pedestal from* The Art and Craft of Garden Making *(1900) by Thomas Mawson*

153

A folding screen provides an interesting canvas to record a memorable garden visit or a trip through garden history. In Paddy Killer's design the panels unfold to reveal the mysteries of Biddulph Grange including the Dahlia Walk, 'China', the Egyptian Pyramid and the Cheshire Cottage

PLACES

Certain places call out to the garden embroiderer because their features, layout and planting are so exceptionally rich in ideas for new projects. Others are exciting because they epitomize the style and mood of a period glimpsed through old needlework. At Ascott, a Rothschild garden in Buckinghamshire, the yew figures of the Edwardian topiary sundial make me think of Ghiordes knot or velvet stitch on a bricking ground, and nearby, at Waddesdon Manor, the lavishly planted bedding schemes in the restored Victorian parterre, outlined in bands of contrasting greenery, suggest opulent ribbonwork cushions. Inside this great treasure house, spectacular seventeenth-century panels, embroidered in swirls of green and amber bugle beads and moss-like chenille, transform a closet into a

glinting grotto with echoes of Marvell's 'green thought in a green shade', setting you off on a different track which alters again as you pass by the Aviary, where the darting birds make kaleidoscopic bargello-like patterns behind the dark grid of wire.

For the embroiderer, garden visiting soon develops an extra dimension, with patterns, colours and textures perceived through needlework-tinted spectacles. At Hatfield House, for example, the knot garden in front of the Old Palace re-creates not only the medley of plants and intricate patterns but the secluded atmosphere of the Elizabethan pleasance, and something of this miraculously survives the hurly-burly of London's traffic in the Tradescant Trust's small but beautifully tended knot garden at the church of St Mary-at-Lambeth, home to the Museum of Garden History. Here you can trace changing

felt collage on a deep green spray-dyed ground.

The features at Biddulph are ingeniously and enticingly separated one from another by trees, shrubberies and rock walls, so visitors find themselves one moment in 'China' admiring a lacquer-red pavilion and bridge framed by bamboos, and the next facing 'Egypt', guarded by stone sphinxes and a massive 'temple' of yew, entered by a tunnel which ends up, not in a pharaoh's tomb, but outside a Cheshire cottage!

Quintessentially Victorian in spirit, Biddulph might be a staging post on a trip through garden history – a series of visits planned to re-experience the shock of the new: the symmetry of the parterres (in the Privy Garden at Hampton Court) after the crowded intricacy of the knots (at Hatfield), and then that symmetry overtaken by the wayward naturalness experienced in the landscape at Stourhead.

Changes in garden styles suggest new methods, and you might find your embroidery interest changing from the tight grid of canvas (so apt for knots) to the freedom of crewel or quilting (ideal for serpentine meanders).

Visiting new places with an embroidery purpose in mind can jolt you out of a needlework rut in the most exciting, pleasurable and often unexpected way. You might plan your route round particular features – fountains and ferneries, say – and return enamoured with topiary and auricula theatres, because a chance shower or trick of evening light suggested threads, stitches or shades unthought of before.

Specialist nurseries may lure you off the planned route, but their delectable rows of plants and imaginative show gardens can germinate further ideas for stitchery as you pick out and group together varieties that are new to you, or that you had always longed to find. Like needlework shops with their dizzying choice of threads and materials, nurseries are heady stuff for enthusiasts, and so too are flower shows where the plants are displayed at eye level, making it easier to assess their merits for the garden – or for embroidery. But beware: too many colours, textures and shapes will result in confusion. 'It can never be repeated too often,' Miss Jekyll wrote in 1901, 'that the very best effects will be made by the simplest means.'

I have no doubt that embroidery refines the eye for the garden, and that the art of gardening generates an endless succession of ideas for needlework – and that this happy cross-fertilization adds greatly to our pleasure and satisfaction, whether we wield a needle or a spade.

garden styles through engravings and book illustrations, see a model of Miss Jekyll's garden at Munstead Wood, jewel-like flowerheads preserved in silver sand in the Elizabethan manner, and a profusion of old tools and Victorian seed packets, zinnias and dahlias, whose intriguing, complex-patterned shapes, set you off in another direction – to Biddulph Grange in Staffordshire perhaps, where the Victorian dahlia walk has been restored to its original glory with old pompoms and cactus varieties displayed in compartments of dark yew, which are suggestive of a folding screen with panels in

Gardens with Features of Special Interest to Embroiderers

These have been listed according to their character, whether original, restored, or introduced in recent times. Most, but not all, of these gardens are open to the public on a regular basis. Always check opening times before setting out.

ELIZABETHAN AND JACOBEAN GARDEN FEATURES
*(those marked * have knots)*

Barnsley House Gardens, nr Cirencester, Glos.* Also potager, laburnum alley, inspiring planting.

Basing House, nr Basingstoke, Berks.*

Broughton Castle, nr Banbury, Oxon.* Fleur-de-lys shaped knot in Ladies' Garden.

Chenies, nr Amersham, Bucks. Mazes, Physic Garden. Also tulips and Victorian-style vegetable garden.

Cranborne Manor Gardens, Cranborne, Dorset.* Mount, also wild and herb gardens.

Doddington Hall, nr Lincoln, Lincs.*

New Place, Stratford-upon-Avon, Warwickshire.*

Hatfield House, Hatfield, Herts.* Also Victorian yew maze and inspiring planting in East and Privy Gardens.

Helmingham Hall, nr Stowmarket, Suffolk.* Double herbaceous borders.

Holdenby House, nr Northampton, Northants.*

Little Moreton Hall, Congleton, Cheshire.* Knot based on a pattern of 1680.

Montacute House, nr Yeovil, Somerset. Elizabethan pavilions, also Stoke Edith hangings.

Moseley Old Hall, Wolverhampton, Staffs.* Knot based on a pattern of 1640, carpenter's work tunnel.

Museum of Garden History, St Mary-at-Lambeth, Lambeth Palace Road, London.*

Sudeley Castle, Winchcombe, Glos.*

The Tudor Garden, Bugle Street, Southampton.*

STUART AND GRAND MANNER FEATURES
*(those marked * have parterres)*

Ashdown House, nr Lambourn, Berks.*

Chelsea Physic Garden, London. Founded as a garden of medicinal herbs in 1673.

Cliveden, nr Taplow, Berks.* Also Japanese Garden.

Chatsworth, nr Bakewell, Derbyshire.* Fountains, cascade.

Erdigg, nr Wrexham, Clwyd. Walled garden with old varieties of fruit, Victorian parterre.

Ham House, Richmond, Surrey.* Wilderness.

Hampton Court Palace, East Molesey, Surrey.* Superlative restoration of the Privy Garden with statues and fountains. Also knot, Great Vine, spring bulbs.

Levens Hall, nr Kendal, Cumbria. Topiary, formal gardens, herb garden.

Melbourne Hall, nr Derby, Derbyshire. Vistas, statues, wrought-iron 'Birdcage' arbour.

Parham Park, Pulborough, Sussex. Embroidered 'Garden of Eden' and examples of 'rockery pools' in the fine collection of seventeenth-century needlework pictures.

Westbury Court, Westbury-on-Severn, Glos. Formal water garden, fruit.

GEORGIAN FEATURES

Castle Howard, nr Malton, N. Yorks. Temples in landscape, also Atlas fountain, rose garden.

Chiswick House, Greater London. Vistas, buildings, statues, lake and cascade.

Harewood House, nr Leeds, W. Yorks. 'Capability' Brown landscape. Also Victorian parterre.

Painshill Park, nr Cobham, Surrey. Grotto, temples, Turkish tent, Chinese Bridge.

Painswick Rococo Garden, nr Stroud, Glos. Rococo buildings.

Rousham House, nr Steeple Aston, Oxon. Ha-ha, vistas, temples, statues.

Royal Botanic Gardens, Kew, Surrey. Pagoda. Also Palm House, sunken herb garden, parterre and mount behind the Dutch Palace.

Stourhead, nr Stourton, Wilts. Lake walk, temples, grotto.

Stowe, nr Buckingham, Bucks. Landscape with temples and buildings.

REGENCY AND VICTORIAN FEATURES

Arley Hall, nr Northwich, Cheshire. Earliest recorded herbaceous borders.

Alton Towers, Alton, Staffs. Pagoda and garden buildings.

Ascott Wing, Bucks. Topiary, sundial.

Audley End, nr Saffron Walden, Essex. Regency flower parterre.

Drummond Castle, nr Crieff, Perthshire. Parterre made in 1830s.

Biddulph Grange, nr Stoke-on-Trent, Staffs. 'China', 'Egypt', dahlia walk.

Kelmscott Manor, nr Farringdon, Oxon. The garden is being restored. Morris embroideries.

Sezincote, nr Moreton-in-Marsh, Glos. Indian-inspired orangery, temple and bridge.

Stancombe Park, Glos. Secret Garden approached through a tunnel, fine planting.

Waddesdon Manor, nr Aylesbury, Bucks. Victorian-style bedding in parterre, also aviary.

Warwick Castle, Warwick. Victorian-style rose garden.

TWENTIETH-CENTURY GARDENS

JEKYLL GARDENS
Hestercombe, nr Taunton, Somerset.

The Manor House, Upton Grey, Hants.

INSPIRING PLANTING
Crathes Castle, Banchory, Grampian.

Great Dixter, E. Sussex. Also topiary, and meadow gardening.

Heale House, Middle Woodford, Wilts. Also Japanese garden and kitchen garden.

Hidcote, Bartrim, Glos. Colour borders and garden rooms.

Marwood Hill Gardens, nr Barnstaple, N. Devon. Water features and bog garden.

Newby Hall, Ripon, Yorks. Herbaceous borders, statue walk, woodland garden.

Royal Horticultural Society's Gardens, Wisley, Surrey. Also wildflower meadow, vegetables and fruit.

Sissinghurst, nr Cranbrook, Kent. Also Cottage and Herb Gardens.

The Garden House, Buckland Monacorum, Devon.

The Priory, Kemerton, Glos. Colour borders.

Tintinhull House, nr Yeovil, Somerset.

White Barns House, Elmstead Market, Essex. Beth Chatto's garden.

VEGETABLES, HERBS AND FRUIT

Burton Agnes Hall, nr Bridlington, Humberside

Fenton House, Hampstead, London. Kitchen garden, seventeenth- and eighteenth-century embroideries.

Hardwick Hall, nr Chesterfield, Derbyshire. Herb garden, Elizabethan embroideries.

Rosemoor, nr Great Torrington, Devon. Potager, vegetable and cottage gardens.

The Lost Garden of Heligan, St Austell, Cornwall. Restored kitchen gardens, also jungle garden.

West Dean, nr Chichester, Sussex. Restored kitchen gardens, glasshouses.

NURSERIES

Hollington Herbs, Wootton Hill, Hants. Knot, herb and paradise gardens.

Langley Boxwood Nursery, Liss, Hants. Topiary shapes.

Stone House Cottage, Kidderminster, Worcs. Imaginative show garden with architectural follies.

Printer's device from Jan Commelin's
Nederlandtze Hesperides, *1676*

Bibliography

Many of the old garden books mentioned in the text can be seen in The Lindley Library of the RHS in London (members only) or in the National Art Library at the Victoria & Albert Museum.

Batey, M. *Regency Gardens*, Shire Publications (1995)
Beck, T. *The Embroiderer's Garden*, David & Charles (1988)
   The Embroiderer's Flowers, David & Charles (1992)
Campbell, S. *Charleston Kedding: a History of Kitchen Gardening*, Ebury Press (1996)
Elliot, B. *Victorian Gardens*, Batsford (1986)
   The Country House Garden from the archives of Country Life 1897–1934, Mitchell Beazley (1995).

Gunn, F. *Lost Gardens of Gertrude Jekyll*, Letts (1991)
Kingsbury, N. *The New Perennial Garden*, Frances Lincoln (1996)
Lord, T. *Gardening at Sissinghurst*, Frances Lincoln, (1995)
Pavord, A. *The New Kitchen Garden*, Dorling Kindersley (1996)
Strong, R. *Small Period Gardens*, Conran Octopus (1992)
Symes, M. *The English Rococo Garden*, Shire Publications, (1991)
Taylor, P. *Planting in Patterns*, Pavilion (1989)
Thacker, C. *The History of Gardens*, Croom Helm (1985)
Van der Horst, A.J. and Jacques, D. *The Gardens of William and Mary*, Croom Helm (1988)

Acknowledgements

I am much indebted to all those who have allowed me to reproduce items from their embroidery collections or garden books, and to the contemporary embroiderers whose work is illustrated. I owe a special 'thank you' to Paddy Killer and Belinda Downes whose drawings embellish the book; I am also most grateful to Dr Brent Elliott and the staff of the Lindley Library, and at David & Charles to Cheryl Brown, Kay Ball, Jane Trollope and Margaret Foster who designed the book.

Most of all I would like to thank Christopher Thacker for his generous and patient help with the garden aspect of my theme.

The illustrations are reproduced by kind permission of the following institutions and individuals. Where no credit is given the illustration is in a private collection.

COLOUR ILLUSTRATIONS

Bodleian Library, 12, 32
Bowes Museum, 27, 87 (on loan from the Earl of Strathmore)
British Library, 40
Burrell Collection, 57, 63
Embroiderers' Guild Museum Collection, 127
English Heritage, 94
Ladies' Work Society, 104
Lane Fine Art, 13
Lindley Library, 101, 107
Mallett, 86
Mayorcas, 18
Metropolitan Museum, New York, 49
National Trust, 2, 68, 73 (photo C. Thacker),74
Parham Park, 23, 47
Society of Antiquaries, 111
C. Thacker photos, 18, 30, 32 top
Victoria & Albert Museum, 4, 31, 36, 85; 9, 24, 37, 42, 43, 55, 59, 61, 69, 80, 83, 69, 97, 102, 109, 126 (photo C. Bishop); 15 (photo P. Barnard)
Witney Antiques, 103

BLACK AND WHITE ILLUSTRATIONS

Ashmolean Museum, 38
Bodleian Library, 97 centre
Christie's, 91
Embroiderers' Guild Museum Collection, 128 left
London Library, 84 top, 100 below, 105 left, 106 top, 116, 123, 124, 129
Metropolitan Museum, New York, 17, 19, 28, 46, 51
Museum of Fine Arts, Boston, 72
National Gallery of Ireland, 93
National Museums and Galleries on Merseyside, 88
National Trust, 34 (photo C. Thacker)
Porcupine's Quill Press, 124 right
Victoria & Albert Museum, 8 top, 16, 20–21, 48 below, 54; 28, 33 top right, 37 top right, 39 bottom, 50 top, 70, 81, 83, 75, 98, 99, 117, 118, 128 bottom right (photo C. Bishop)

Detail of the frontispiece of Robert Turner's Botanologia: The British Physician, *1664*

Index

Decorative motif from The Embroideress *c.1930*